KU-023-789

PORK

for Denver Phil

for Tina & Jack Simon

First published in Great Britain in 2013 by
Kyle Books, an imprint of Kyle Cathie Ltd
192–198 Vauxhall Bridge Road
London SW1V 1DX
general.enquiries@kylebooks.com
www.kylebooks.com

10 9 8 7 6 5 4 3 2

ISBN 978 0 85783 101 9

Text © 2013 Phil Vickery and Simon Boddy
Design © 2013 Kyle Books
Photographs © 2013 Peter Cassidy
Illustrations © 2013 K-Fai Steele

Phil Vickery and Simon Boddy are hereby
identified as the authors of this work in
accordance with Section 77 of the Copyright,
Designs and Patents Act 1988.

All rights reserved. No reproduction, copy or
transmission of this publication may be made
without written permission. No paragraph of
this publication may be reproduced, copied
or transmitted save with written permission
or in accordance with the provisions of the
Copyright Act 1956 (as amended). Any person
who does any unauthorised act in relation to
this publication may be liable to criminal
prosecution and civil claims for damages.

Editor **Judith Hannam**
Editorial Assistant **Tara O'Sullivan**
Copy Editor **Jo Richardson**
Designer **Helen Bratby**
Photographer **Peter Cassidy**
Illustrator **K-Fai Steele**
Food Stylist **Mima Sinclair**
Prop Stylist **Iris Bromet**
Production **Nic Jones and David Hearn**

A Cataloguing in Publication record for this
title is available from the British Library.

Colour reproduction by ALTA London
Printed and bound in China by Toppan
Leefung Printing Ltd

Important note The information contained
in this book is intended as a general guide
to curing and smoking and is based on the
authors' own experimentation, experience
and research. Neither the authors nor the
publishers can be held responsible for the
consequences of the application or
misapplication of any of the information
or ideas presented in this book.

PORK

Preparing, curing & cooking all that's possible from a pig

BY PHIL VICKERY & SIMON BODDY
PHOTOGRAPHY PETER CASSIDY

KYLE BOOKS

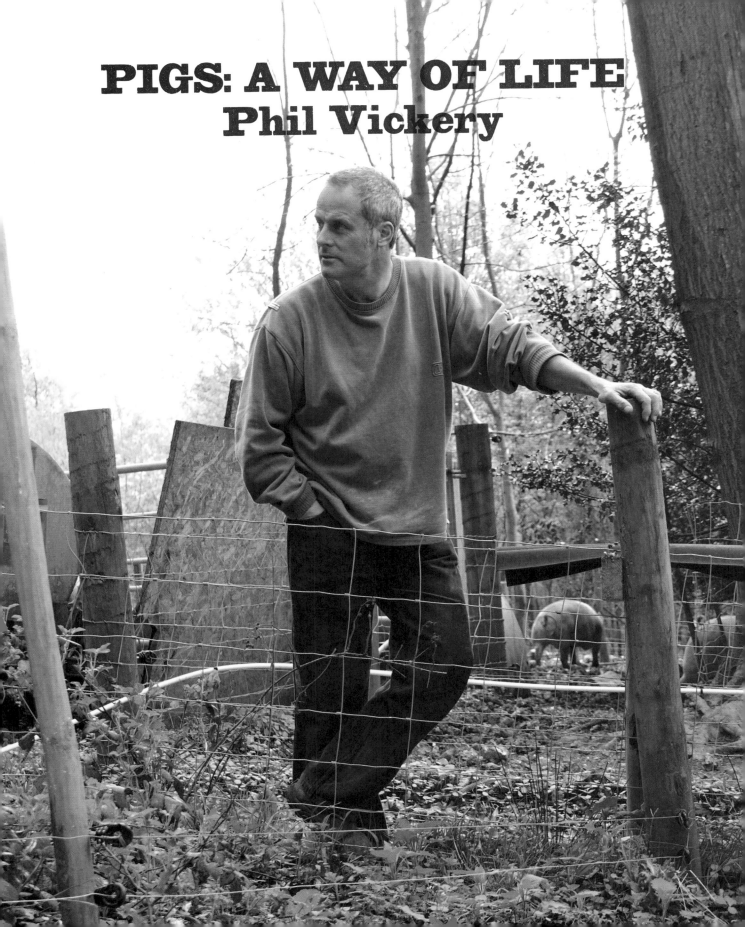

PIGS: A WAY OF LIFE
Phil Vickery

y fascination with pigs started at an early age. I remember vividly my father buying a half pig from a local farmer and cutting it up at home to pop into the freezer for the winter months. We lived in the country, just outside Folkestone in Kent. I'm sure this was not an every-day occurrence, but it seemed quite normal to us. It was the first time I had seen a dead animal ever, let alone in the house. My father would not only cut and tie the whole thing up but also use all the extremities. Even to this day, like my brothers and me, he adores trotters and always asks me to get him a couple when I go to the butchery. Another of his great favourites was brawn. I can still see it now, a quivering jellified mould of chunks of pig head, tongue and brain. He would make it in a Pyrex bowl and turn it out onto a white enamel plate with a dark blue edge. That was tea, along with bread and sometimes piccalilli.

The first book I ever read on cooking was given to me by the local church hall caretaker. I reckon I must have been eight or nine, and I had never shown any real interest in cooking before, so my mum says. I'm not quite sure why he gave it to me. I think he was trying to keep me occupied while my father helped out clearing up after a jumble sale. The 1936 edition of *Warne's Everyday Cookery*, it really fired me up with its wonderful colour and black and white plates of elaborate dishes and preparation methods from chefs. Flicking through it some 40 or more years later, there in the front I found a recipe for my dad's brawn, written down by me, along with another of his favourites, bread pudding.

The farmer who supplied my dad was a lovely man called George King. He was a big man, quietly spoken and always wearing a flat hat. His son Andrew helped him out on the farm and his mum ran the small shop. My elder brother Chris worked on the farm on a Saturday, helping out with various jobs, and one late-summer day he asked me if I would like to help spud picking. This entailed walking up and down the field picking up potatoes that had been spun out of the dry ground by the tractor. It was hard, back-breaking work, but I did enjoy it. We would get 50p a sack (56lb in those days), with a few bags of fruit thrown in and a small bottle of milk straight from the cow for our cornflakes.

I progressed from spud picking to feeding and watering the pigs. It took a good hour and involved jumping in and out of a long row of pigsties. George named each sty, and the first one I remember was called Barrel's, then Green Doors, The Piggery and finally Kathmandu on the end, as it was the furthest away. We would grind the barley or wheat for feeding the pigs in a large mill with a huge hopper, then mix it with a pre-bought feed. On some Saturdays, a large van would appear carrying 20 or so flour bags crammed full of bread, cakes, buns and doughnuts from a local baker. Some were still good to eat and Andrew and I would stuff ourselves. The pigs, needless to say, would gorge themselves too. They also had great names such as Gertrude, a lovely Saddleback, and Queenie, a Duroc cross. Albert the boar would make sure they were all kept happy and in pig. Occasionally you would get a runt or a pig that wasn't quite right; Wibbly and Ted were classic examples. Wibbly walked sideways and had a constant shake, probably due to brain damage caused by her mother laying on her, but she was lovely, affectionate and such a character. Ted was a boar runt with a large belly that almost dragged on the ground and a constant sniffle. Wibbly and Ted became good friends and lived in the barn, from where they would roam the farm. Both, I have to say, made great pork, probably because they really were free range.

Those were good times – no *E. coli*, no restrictions on feed, no hassle and above all great-tasting pork. This was small-scale production and way before I had even heard of intensive farming. I'm sure it existed, but the focus then was not on feeding regimes and state-of-the-art quick-growing feed but on well-reared, good-quality, delicious meat. In fact, all the hotels and restaurants I ever worked in always had a 'pig man', who once a week would take away large bins filled with the leftover food. From there it was boiled, sieved, cooled and fed to pigs. That has all stopped due to very strict regulation. My belief is that we should return to those days because thousands of tonnes of perfectly good food are now being tipped into landfill. A lot of commercial pig food is bulked out with cooked, dry bakery products like George used to use, so to me there is no difference between that and 'waste' food. But for this to work of course, the collection, cooking and use of the food must be properly regulated and controlled, ensuring no raw meat or fish products are allowed to enter the food chain.

One thing I did learn with George was the cycle of pig rearing. Piglets were born, weaned off, fed and fattened and then sold. It was not by any means a large-scale operation, but it taught me that well-reared, well-looked-after and well-fed pigs produce great-tasting end products. If you are about to embark on pig keeping or production, you have to be committed, in my eyes, to humane ways of rearing and housing, fresh water and good feed and a peaceful existence. You also have to follow the process right through from cute weaners to the slaughterhouse. Yes, the final stage is unpleasant, but only then can you fully understand the importance of the whole cycle.

Slaughtering is not a pleasant experience, as I have said, but all the slaughterhouses I have been to treat the animals with great care and attention. A stressed animal is no good to anyone; adrenalin can cause havoc in fresh meat if the animal is not properly looked after. Simon, my butcher and co-author of this book, once called me to say that a pig carcass was like jelly due to adrenalin. I would much rather eat meat that I know has been reared and treated correctly and humanely from start to finish. I have, over the years, dabbled in pork production and gone to great lengths to ensure that all my animals had a good life.

I often get asked about rare and old pig breeds, and which offer the best and highest meat yield, lowest fat content and so on. To me, there were and still are some fabulous breeds around. However, one of the main reasons some are no longer with us is because they either have a very low meat yield or are too fatty. I personally like Oxford Sandy and Black, Berkshire and a cross between Pietrain, Duroc and Middle White. Gloucester Old Spot is widely used these days by chefs, along with Tamworth, but it really depends on what you are going to do with the end product. The issue of pork's fat content always rears its head though, and the press is full of shock-horror stories of this most demonised of food products. Some research even suggests that pork fat can actually be good for you in certain circumstances, and lean pork has less fat per kilo than cottage cheese. The supermarkets have to take a little of the blame here. They say that their customers want a very small amount of fat on their joints and cuts, whereas those I talk to want more fat – not a lot, but slightly more. So I think it has a lot to do with a quicker turnaround of product; the longer you leave pigs to fatten, the more they cost you in feed.

From a chef's point of view, pork is an incredibly versatile meat. I always say that you can pretty much marry any flavour profile to it. Spices work well with pork; take for instance a pork vindaloo where the meat melds with the spicy fragrance and doesn't overpower the final dish. Sweet fruits such as mango, roasted pears and raspberries are perfect, but equally sharp fruits such as blackcurrants, rhubarb and lime or lemon also seem to go naturally with it. Some fish works well with pork too; lobster, prawns, scallops and even salmon make ideal partners. Cream, mustard, vinegars, oils and many herbs are all fine with pork – it's truly fail-safe.

Years ago, all over the world, many families kept a pig that was fattened for the lean winter months, including here in the UK. The pig spent spring and summer gorging itself and when the time came provided the family with much-needed, highly nutritious food. Every part of the animal was prepared and eaten fresh, or preserved. Salting and drying was the most popular preserving method. Preserving it in its own fat, or confit, is still practised today by many chefs and restaurants, as it results in a very long shelf life.

Our European friends produce a dazzling array of preserved meats and it was on a filming trip in the south of Spain that I realised how far behind we are in the UK. I flew to Seville and then drove up to Aracena in the western Andalucian countryside to meet Miguel. He was responsible for overseeing the PR that surrounds arguably the world's best air-dried ham, jamón Ibérico. We toured the area – incredibly, the size of Holland – that produces these wonderful, happy and, yes, tasty pigs. They feast on acorns and put on roughly a third of their weight in just three months. They are amazingly clever, deftly removing the outside husk of the acorn before eating the centre and spitting out the rest. At about one year old they are rounded up and processed, packed in salt and then left to hang for many months until the ham has produced a fantastic unrivalled sweetness. Some hams are eaten after only a few months but others are hung for as long as five years, all controlled by human eye, feel and expertise. On saying goodbye to Miguel, we shook hands and he said 'Trouble is Phil, you can't do this in the UK.' On the plane I fell asleep but after a few minutes woke up and thought about what Miguel had said to me. Why can't we? We have pigs, we have salt and we can mimic the temperature and, more importantly, the humidity.

So about ten years ago I bought some land and practised producing ham, buying what I thought were the right breed and rearing them. What a disaster – mouldy meat, tough, too dry, awful. I tried again, and failed again. I remember going to the abattoir and the farmers slow hand clapping me as I tried to reverse a trailer. A good friend of mine, Peter Gott, once said to me, 'Show me your hands'. I duly did and he said, 'You're not a real farmer, you haven't got enough s**t on your hands.' Of course he was right, but he did agree to help me. I was about to give up when I was introduced to Simon Boddy, a big, gruff butcher with a disdain for chefs; I can't put in print what he called them. He didn't trust me and made that very clear. It turned out he was a master in curing and preserving. We became good friends and partners, and I found somebody that shared my passion for pigs and cured meats. His knowledge and experience is second to none, and his dedication to his work borders on obsession. We still josh each other about those early days. When I decided to write a book on pork, I simply had to have Simon on board to help me. So here is the product of probably 60 years' sheer hard work and dedication. Yes, Miguel was right to a certain extent, but watch out, we're catching up!

PORK: A WAY OF LIFE
Simon Boddy

Sus scrofa domesticus, more commonly known as the domestic pig, has always been considered to be a subspecies of the wild boar. There is archaeological evidence, found in the Tigris basin in eastern Turkey, to suggest that the pig was domesticated from the wild boar as early as 13000–12700 BC, a process achieved by our ancestors with relative ease due to the adaptable and omnivorous nature of the creature. Wild boar were indigenous to Western Europe, including Great Britain, and were widespread by the Middle Ages. There is some debate as to whether wild boar populations were locally domesticated or the modern European domestic pig was produced by crossing native wild boars with domesticated Asian pigs. In the late 18th century, Chinese pigs were brought to the UK, and in 1830 a grey-black boar and sow were imported from Italy by a Lord Weston. These and other foreign breeds were introduced to improve the variety, quality and quantity of the meat. Although there is not much authentic information available to explain how our breeds developed, I suspect that the breeds we know today owe a fair amount to this ancestry.

Although I have worked with pork for nearly 30 years, my real fascination began about 15 years ago. I had just lost quite a big customer and was looking for ways to replace the turnover. The pork industry in the UK at that time was on its knees and it was really tough for pig farmers. It was suggested to me that we could perhaps offer a service to farmers that would increase the value of their pigs, namely turning them into cured products such as bacon and sausages. I contacted *Farmers Weekly* and they ran an article on it. We started to get enquiries fairly quickly, and before long we began to process some pigs. I have to say that the venture exceeded my expectations and with the advent of farmers' markets in the late 1990s it turned into a whole new career. Along with the extra business I started to learn about the various pig breeds and how different they all are.

By far the most popular pig breeds are what we generically call the rare breeds, which include the Gloucester Old Spot, Tamworth, Large Black, Middle White, Berkshire, Oxford Sandy and Black and the Saddleback. Unfortunately, I have absolutely no affection for any of these breeds. There is a massive misconception that rare breeds provide the most flavoursome pork and the tastiest bacon and sausages, which is frankly an absolute load of codswallop. The reason these breeds are rare is because from a commercial point of view nobody wants them, and certainly not me! I mention the word 'commercial' because the bulk of pork (at least in the UK) is produced commercially and you will hear no mention of a rare breed on a commercial pig unit – but the term you will hear is 'hybrid'.

With pressure from consumers to have less fat and more meat, and pressure from the multiples to have cheaper pork, we have over the years seen pig-improvement companies evolve and develop hybrid strains of pig to satisfy such demands. These companies will take certain breeds of pig and, using applied pig genetic development techniques, produce strains of breeding stock that fulfil the most stringent of requirements, i.e. a pig with a long lean back and double-muscled hams.

When I met Phil, the first pigs we processed together were Sandy and Black crosses. The estimated usable lean meat of these pigs was somewhere between 30 and 40 per cent, which is simply not good enough for what we wanted to achieve. Don't get me wrong, the meat we did get was fantastic, but there was just not enough of it. I introduced Phil to a customer of mine who happened to be a pig farmer producing outdoor-reared weaners for one of the leading supermarkets. These pigs were a hybrid specifically bred to produce lean, well-muscled carcasses and could be kept on a free-range system. The biggest proportion of the breeding came from the Large White and Landrace, with Duroc and Hampshire providing the hardiness and intramuscular marbling, and Pietrain the muscle conformation. Our first batch of hybrid pigs went into some fenced-off woodland that we had access to and they were allowed to act like pigs should act – foraging and uprooting everything in their path – as well as being fed a feed ration with all the components in it to keep them healthy and fatten them for slaughter. They were nine months old at slaughter and as carcasses were just what we wanted to produce some wonderful charcuterie. After that, there was no looking back!

CHAPTER 1 Shoulder & ribs

The front end of any animal, especially the shoulder, often gets a bit forgotten. Yes, it's the fattiest part and when you balance out the meat to fat ratio it is far higher than, say, the loin, fillet or even gammon. This, though, can be an advantage. A rolled shoulder of pork, for instance, will be delicious, even if slightly overdone, because the amount of fat it contains means it is constantly basted throughout the duration of cooking. The meat from the shoulder is also great for pot-roasting, braising or stewing, plus it makes excellent burgers. A pork burger can be very dry, but one using minced shoulder will be deliciously succulent because it's roughly 15–20 per cent fat. Neck fillet, cut from the top shoulder, can be equally delicious when lightly grilled, sautéed or barbecued and it is not often used.

Simon always says that good salami is best made from carefully butchered meat from the shoulder. When we make salami together he 'seams out' all the individual muscles (cuts where they are attached to each other or to the bone) and then mixes them with a proportion of good-quality fat. Sausages taste good primarily because the meat has a good fat content; remove that and the meat tastes dull. A lot of the sausages you can buy are made using any old rubbish left over, but we take great care to get the right balance of good-quality meat, fat content and seasoning.

Ribs have become extremely trendy over the past few years. Almost every café/brasserie/diner serves them in some way, shape or form, which is not surprising as there is something enormously satisfying about tucking into a rack of glistening, full-flavoured, sticky ribs – real finger food! I was lucky enough to spend some time in North Carolina learning how to prepare and smoke them properly. The most important rule to remember is to cook ribs long and slow in a moist environment – then the meat will fall off the bone. Yes, they are essentially a by-product and would normally be thrown away, but our American friends have turned them into high-end cooking. All over the Southern states there are cookery competitions focused on ribs, and they spend hours – sometimes days – perfecting their recipes. I have tried to make mine a little more user-friendly so they are easy to cook, but no less delicious. – Phil

Hand of pork braised with dried blueberries & elderberries

I USE ELDERBERRIES THAT I DRY MYSELF AND IT'S A PERFECT WAY OF KEEPING THEM FOR THE WINTER MONTHS. I HAVE NOT SEEN THEM AVAILABLE TO PURCHASE COMMERCIALLY YET. HOWEVER, IF YOU DON'T HAVE ELDERBERRIES, ANY DRIED RED FRUIT WILL DO. EIGHT HEADS WILL PRODUCE ABOUT 350G FRESH BERRIES, AND ONCE DRIED THEY WILL REDUCE IN VOLUME BY ABOUT HALF. I HAVE SOME AT HOME THAT ARE A YEAR OLD. TO DRY THE BERRIES, SPREAD OUT ON A NON-STICK BAKING TRAY AND PLACE IN A VERY COOL OVEN, SAY 110°C/GAS ¼, FOR ABOUT 6–7 HOURS. YOU CAN USE A DEHYDRATOR TO DRY THEM IN LESS TIME. THE SAME PROCESS APPLIES TO DRYING FRESH BLUEBERRIES, BUT YOU CAN BUY SEMI-DRIED BLUEBERRIES FROM SUPERMARKETS THAT ARE PRETTY GOOD. ONE OTHER TIP I PICKED UP IN HUNGARY – NEVER ADD PAPRIKA TO HOT OIL, AS IT WILL BURN, TURN BITTER AND LOSE ITS PERFUME. IF YOU CAN, ALWAYS ADD ONCE ALL THE LIQUID HAS GONE IN.

Serves 4   Preparation time 20 minutes   Cooking time about 2 hours, plus standing

4 tablespoons vegetable oil
1 large onion, very finely chopped
1kg hand of pork or shoulder, rind and fat removed, cut into 3cm pieces
3 tablespoons plain flour
1 glass Madeira
1 glass water
10g pork or chicken stock cube, crumbled
2 tablespoons caster sugar
1½ tablespoons smoked paprika
2 tablespoons dried elderberries
2 tablespoons dried blueberries
3 tablespoons pearl barley
salt and freshly ground black pepper

TO SERVE
200g thick Greek yogurt
6 tablespoons chopped fresh flat-leaf parsley

✱ Preheat the oven to 160°C/Gas 4.

✱ Put a large ovenproof pan with a tight-fitting lid on the hob and heat the vegetable oil over a low heat. Add the onion and cook for 5 minutes to soften slightly.

✱ Mix the pork and flour together well in a bowl. Add to the pan and brown all over, then add the Madeira, water and stock cube and mix well. Stir in the sugar, paprika, dried berries and barley.

✱ Season well with salt and pepper, mix thoroughly and just bring to the boil. Immediately cover the pan with the lid, then transfer to the oven and cook for 1 hour 45 minutes.

✱ Remove from the oven and leave to stand for 20 minutes. Stir in the yogurt and serve scattered with the chopped parsley. It's as simple as that.

Roast pork with white wine, oranges & oregano

I FIRST COOKED THIS DISH SOME 20 YEARS AGO, AND THE COMBINATION OF FRESH ORANGE AND PUNGENT OREGANO WORKS VERY WELL INDEED WITH PORK. I ALSO REVEAL HERE HOW TO ACHIEVE PERFECT CRACKLING EVERY TIME – IT REALLY IS VERY STRAIGHTFORWARD. ALL YOU NEED TO SERVE WITH THIS DISH IS A LARGE BOWL OF NEW POTATOES AND SOME PURPLE SPROUTING BROCCOLI OR EVEN A FEW ASPARAGUS SPEARS.

Serves 6   Preparation time 20 minutes   Cooking time 1 hour 40 minutes, plus resting

1kg boned shoulder of pork, tied
salt and freshly ground black pepper

SAUCE
1 large glass dry white wine
½ x 10g chicken stock cube, crumbled (to add a little extra flavour to the sauce)
275ml fresh orange juice
2 teaspoons caster sugar
2 teaspoons fresh or 1 tablespoon dried oregano
1 heaped tablespoon arrowroot or cornflour

* Preheat the oven to 190°C/Gas 5.

* Season the joint well with salt and pepper, then place on a piece of scrunched-up foil in a roasting tray and pop in the oven. I normally cook this size joint for about 1 hour 20 minutes.

* Remove the roasting tray from the oven. Cut off the strings around the joint, remove all the crackling and place, inner-side up, on a baking tray. Cover the joint with foil and leave to rest for a further 20 minutes before you eat. This helps the meat relax and become a lot juicier.

* While the meat is resting, place the baking tray with the crackling in the oven, turn the oven up to 220°C/Gas 7 and cook until it turns crispy and well browned. This should take about 20 minutes.

* Meanwhile, tip off all the fat from the roasting tray, add the wine and swirl around to remove any crispy bits from the tin. Spoon into a saucepan and bring to the boil. Add the stock cube, orange juice, sugar and oregano, then bring back to the boil. Cook for about 5 minutes to reduce slightly and for the stock cube to dissolve, then re-season.

* Blend the arrowroot or cornflour with a little cold water until smooth, then stir into the boiling sauce – it will thicken straight away. Keep warm and covered.

* To serve, slice the pork, spoon over a little of the sauce and top with a piece of crackling.

Pot roast shoulder of pork with sauerkraut, cider vinegar & mustard

ONE OF SIMON'S GREAT IDEAS, THE SUCCULENCE THAT COMES FROM BRINING THE MEAT FIRST MAKES A MASSIVE DIFFERENCE AND IS REALLY WORTHWHILE. THIS CUT ALSO PARTICULARLY LENDS ITSELF TO POT ROASTING WITH A VERY SMALL AMOUNT OF LIQUID. THE CARAWAY AND TARRAGON, TWO FLAVOURS VERY MUCH USED IN GERMAN CURES, COMPLETE THE DISH PERFECTLY. SO DELICIOUS – YOU CAN'T STOP EATING IT!

Serves 4   Preparation time 25 minutes, plus 12 hours brining   Cooking time 2 hours

1kg rolled shoulder of pork
2 tablespoons vegetable oil
2 medium onions, finely chopped
2 garlic cloves, chopped
2 teaspoons caraway seeds
3 tablespoons Dijon or sweet mustard
100ml cider vinegar
100ml pork or strong chicken stock (or 2 x 10g stock cubes)
400g jar sauerkraut, drained well
1 tablespoon cornflour or arrowroot
2 tablespoons roughly chopped fresh tarragon
salt and freshly ground black pepper

BRINE
500ml water
50g cooking salt
2 garlic cloves, crushed
1 tablespoon caraway seeds
1 sprig of fresh thyme
1 teaspoon freshly ground black pepper
1 tablespoon brown sugar

✽ Make the brine according to the instructions on page 45. Soak the pork joint in the brine (make sure it is covered) for 12 hours or overnight, then dry off with kitchen paper before roasting. Rinse the meat well.

✽ Preheat the oven to 160°C/Gas 3.

✽ Heat a tablespoon of vegetable oil in a deep, lidded pan big enough to hold the pork. Add the onions, garlic and caraway seeds and soften for 10 minutes, but do not brown.

✽ Next add the mustard, vinegar, stock and sauerkraut, and season well with pepper. Bring to the boil and check the seasoning, adding salt if necessary (there will already be some from the sauerkraut and the stock cubes).

✽ Add the brined pork and cover with a tight fitting lid or foil. Simmer for 5 minutes, then transfer into the preheated oven. Cook for 1 hour 30 minutes.

✽ Remove from the oven and take off the lid. The aroma will be amazing. Carefully lift out the pork using two forks and place in a bowl. The meat should be soft and yielding but not falling apart. Remove the strings and carefully slice off the skin. Wrap the joint tightly in foil and set aside to rest. Place the skin on a foil-lined baking tray and put back in the oven, skin side down. Increase the heat to 220°C/Gas 7 and cook until the skin is nice and crispy, about 15–20 minutes.

✽ Meanwhile, strain the sauerkraut/onion mixture and reboil the stock that's left. I sometimes thicken it slightly by adding 1 tablespoon cornflour or arrowroot slaked in 3 tablespoons cold water. Finally, add the chopped fresh tarragon.

✽ Serve the pork thickly sliced with the sauerkraut and tarragon stock.

My fragrant pork vindaloo

SOME PEOPLE THINK OF VINDALOO AS A VERY HOT CURRY, WHICH CAN CERTAINLY BE THE CASE HERE IN THE UK, BUT IT SHOULD IN FACT BE A FRAGRANT DISH, MILD YET PUNGENT IN CHARACTER. THIS REQUIRES A COMPLEX BALANCE OF FLAVOURINGS, AS THE LENGTHY LIST OF INGREDIENTS BELOW SHOWS. BUT DON'T BE PUT OFF – THE SECRET IS SIMPLY TO ENSURE THAT THE SPICE MIX IS CAREFULLY PREPARED FOR THE BEST RESULTS.

Serves 4–6   Preparation time 1 hour standing/soaking   Cooking time about 2 hours

750g shoulder of pork (I like to include some extra fat), cut into large cubes
4 tablespoons caster sugar
2 tablespoons salt

SAUCE
4 large dried red chillies
2 tablespoons ground cumin
2 tablespoons ground coriander
2 teaspoons coriander seeds, crushed
5 teaspoons garam masala
2 teaspoons ground fenugreek
6 tablespoons vegetable oil
6 garlic cloves, chopped
2 tablespoons finely chopped fresh ginger
3 onions, finely sliced

8 ripe tomatoes, chopped
2 tablespoons tomato purée
2 tablespoons smoked paprika
20 curry leaves
300ml tomato juice
2 tablespoons cider vinegar
a pinch or two of caster sugar, to taste
salt and freshly ground black pepper

✱ Preheat the oven to 180°C/Gas 4.

✱ Put the cubed pork into a bowl, add the sugar and salt and mix well. Cover and leave to stand in a cool place for 1 hour, mixing occasionally.

✱ Meanwhile, place the chillies in 100ml warm water and leave to soak for 30 minutes. Drain the chillies, reserving the water, and then chop them up to make a paste – a pestle and mortar is good here, but still chop them finely first.

✱ Gently toast the cumin and ground and crushed coriander in a large frying pan, then stir in the garam masala and fenugreek off the heat and leave to cool.

✱ After 1 hour, rinse the pork well in a colander to remove all the sugar and salt, then pat dry with kitchen paper.

✱ Heat half the oil in a large ovenproof pan with a tight-fitting lid over a low heat, add the garlic and ginger and cook until well coloured. Then add the onions and brown well.

✱ Next add the tomatoes, tomato purée, paprika, curry leaves, tomato juice, vinegar, sugar and salt and pepper. Stir well and then add the spices, chilli paste and reserved water and cook down for about 8–10 minutes until the sauce is nice and thick.

✱ Heat the remaining oil in a separate large pan and brown the pork quickly, in batches if necessary, then add to the sauce. Check the seasoning. Bring to a simmer, then cover with the lid, pop into the oven and cook for 1 hour 30 minutes. Check at that point – the meat should be tender and succulent, but not overcooked. When ready, serve with boiled rice.

Crispy pork salad with maple syrup scratchings & lemon

THIS IS A GREAT DISH THAT MAKES MINCED PORK GO A LONG WAY. THE SPICES, COUPLED WITH THE RELATIVELY HIGH FAT CONTENT OF THE PORK, HELP TO MAKE A REALLY TASTY SALAD, WITH THE RECOOKED SCRATCHINGS ADDING A NICE SWEET, CRISPY EDGE.

Serves 4   Preparation time 20 minutes   Cooking time 20–25 minutes

500g minced pork, slightly fattier is better – any cut
 from the shoulder is perfect
1 teaspoon salt
1 tablespoon Chinese five-spice powder
½ tablespoon ground cumin
2 tablespoons vegetable oil
salt and freshly ground black pepper

SCRATCHINGS
200g pork scratchings (alternatively, crispy bacon pieces
 are just as good), shop bought or see page 188
4 tablespoons maple syrup

DRESSING
4 tablespoons runny honey
finely grated zest and juice of 2 large lemons
3 tablespoons olive oil
2 tablespoons dark soy sauce
2 tablespoons nam pla (Thai fish sauce)
1 teaspoon caster sugar

SALAD
1 Cos (Romaine) or Iceberg lettuce, very finely shredded
1 small bunch of radishes, washed, green shoots left on
 and thinly sliced
1 small bag watercress

✱ Preheat the oven to 200°C/Gas 6.

✱ Put the scratchings into a non-stick ovenproof frying pan, spoon over the maple syrup and mix well. Pop into the oven and cook for 10 minutes, stirring occasionally, until nicely browned and all the maple syrup has been soaked up. Take care, as they will easily burn.

✱ Remove the pan from the oven and leave the scratchings to cool. They will stick together while they are cooling, so break them up.

✱ Meanwhile, put the pork, salt, five-spice and cumin into a bowl and mix well.

✱ Heat a large non-stick frying pan on the hob and add the vegetable oil, then add the pork mixture. As the pork heats up, break it up with a wooden spoon or spatula until the meat is all loose and cooking nicely. Take care here – it's a bit fiddly, but well worth the effort to break up all the small strands of mince. You will find that the meat starts to

boil, but this is no problem and quite normal, especially with vacuum-packed meat. Let the mince boil, stirring all the time. After a few minutes, the water will evaporate and the pork will start to cook in the small amount of oil and the fat from the meat.

✱ After a further 5 minutes, the meat will brown nice and evenly. Once really browned and crispy, spoon it into a colander over a bowl to catch the oil and fat. Sprinkle with a little salt and pepper.

✱ Next make the dressing. Put all the dressing ingredients into a bowl. Add a little salt and pepper and whisk it all together well.

✱ Put the lettuce, radishes and watercress into a salad bowl, spoon over the dressing and mix well but carefully. Add the warm crispy pork and again mix well but carefully.

✱ Pile the salad onto four serving plates and top with the crunchy scratchings. Serve straight away.

Succulent pork with plums, sugar & onions

I HAVE USED THIS RECIPE BEFORE IN MY OTHER BOOKS, BUT IT'S SO GOOD THAT I JUST HAVE TO REPEAT IT. YES, BEFORE I GET READERS' LETTERS, YOU DO ADD THE PORK TO THE BUBBLING CARAMEL. IT REALLY IS SO EASY AND THE PLUMS MAKE A GREAT SAUCE ONCE COOKED DOWN. ANY FRUIT WOULD WORK WELL HERE; SO TRY APPLES, PEARS, MANGO AND EVEN KIWI FRUIT.

Serves 4–6   Preparation time 15 minutes   Cooking time about 2 hours 15 minutes

80g caster sugar
1.2kg shoulder of pork, rind removed but fat left on, cut into 6cm chunks
2 onions, roughly chopped
3 tablespoons Worcestershire sauce
3 tablespoons dark soy sauce
4 tablespoons lemon juice
2 x 10g chicken stock cubes, crumbled
12 ripe British plums, halved and stoned
200g black pudding, sliced
225g frozen peas, cooked
1 tablespoon arrowroot or cornflour
salt and freshly ground black pepper

* Preheat the oven to 180°C/Gas 4.

* Put a large ovenproof pan with a tight-fitting lid on the hob and heat the sugar in the pan over a medium heat.

* Meanwhile, dry the pork chunks on kitchen paper – the drier they are, the better. Season the pork well with salt and pepper.

* Stir the melting sugar with a wooden spoon until you have a thick caramel. If the sugar starts to burn, you can add a small amount of water, which will slow the process. Add the pork to the caramel, mix well and cook for 2–3 minutes.

* Stir in the onions, sauces, lemon juice and stock cubes, and mix well. Bring to the boil, then add the plums, black pudding and a little salt, and again mix well.

* Bring back to the boil, then cover with the lid and transfer to the oven. Cook for 2 hours and then check to see if the meat is cooked through and very tender.

* Once the meat is ready, stir in the peas. Mix the arrowroot or cornflour with 2–3 tablespoons water, stir into the pan and warm through on the hob. Serve with boiled, slightly crushed new potatoes.

SOUS VIDE

Sous vide is the French for 'under vacuum' and is a method of cooking meat or vegetables for longer periods of time and at much lower temperatures than normal. It ensures that whatever you are cooking achieves the same level of 'doneness' at the centre as it does on the outside. Meat in particular remains exceptionally juicy if cooked in this way. It has become extremely popular over the last few years and if used in the right context is a fantastic way to cook meat, especially pork. I was shown the basics of this method on a visit to Belgium about 12 years ago with one of my ingredients suppliers. It was absolutely fascinating and I subsequently started using some of the techniques in my own business.

During the summer there is nothing nicer, weather permitting, than eating barbecued spare ribs with a wonderful sticky sauce. However, when simply grilled over charcoal for a short amount of time, spare ribs can be one of the toughest things you could ever put in your mouth. Precooking them using the sous-vide method will give you some of the most tender spare ribs imaginable. You will need access to a vacuum packer and a sous-vide water bath or steam combination oven to do it to the letter, but there is a way you can do it at home without either. – Simon

St Louis cut spare ribs

I FIRST HAD THESE AT A RIB SHACK IN ST LUCIA WHILE ON HOLIDAY, AND AMAZING IS THE ONLY DESCRIPTION I CAN GIVE THEM. USING THE SOUS-VIDE METHOD OF COOKING IS THE CLOSEST I HAVE COME TO RECREATING THAT MELT-IN-THE-MOUTH TEXTURE.

Serves 4–5   Preparation time 8–10 hours

1 rack St Louis cut spare ribs
(these are cut from the belly so are rectangular in shape,
making every rib the same length and thickness)

✱ On the inner rib side of the rack is a very fine, thin, gossamer-like skin coating the ribs. This must be removed before cooking or the ribs will be tough as old boots. It's very easy to remove – take a sharp knife and, from the top of the last rib bone, scrape the skin away from the cut bone end. It should come away easily. Once you have enough to pull away, get a piece of kitchen towel, grab hold of the skin and pull. It will tear away easily along the whole inside of the rib cage. Then continue with your chosen method below.

THE PROPER METHOD

✱ Place the rack in a vacuum cooking bag and vacuum seal. Place the bag in a sous vide water bath or steam combination oven and cook for 8–10 hours at 72°C.

✱ After cooking, chill very quickly in iced water and refrigerate until you are ready to barbecue or grill them (see page 34).

THE IMPROVISED METHOD

✱ Wrap the rib rack tightly in foil or clingfilm and place on a roasting rack in a roasting tray with 1cm water in the bottom. Wrap the tray and rib package tightly in foil to create a kind of tent.

✱ Set your oven to its lowest temperature – 80–90°C if possible – and cook for 8–10 hours. After cooking, refrigerate until you are ready to barbecue or grill them (see page 34).

Chinese spare ribs ⇒

Chinese spare ribs

A STAPLE IN OUR HOUSE, I LOVE THE SPICES ON THESE RIBS. AGAIN, THIS IS A VERY EASY DISH TO MAKE, BUT MAKE SURE YOU KEEP COATING THE RIBS WELL WITH THE MARINADE. I USE SPARE RIBS THAT ARE CUT FROM THE BELLY SO THAT THEY HAVE MUCH MORE MEAT ON THEM, AS OPPOSED TO THE BABY BACK ONES CUT FROM THE TOP OF THE RIBS TOWARDS THE LOIN.

Serves 4   Preparation time 2 hours or overnight marinating   Cooking time 1–2 hours simmering, 45 minutes–1 hour roasting

1kg whole racks large spare ribs, full of meat
10g beef stock cube, crumbled

MARINADE
6 tablespoons tomato ketchup
4 tablespoons hoisin sauce
4 tablespoons dark soy sauce
2 tablespoons runny honey
2 tablespoons Chinese rice wine or dry sherry
1 tablespoon sweet chilli sauce
1 teaspoon sesame oil
2 garlic cloves, grated
1½ tablespoons grated fresh ginger
¼ teaspoon Chinese five-spice powder

✱ On the inner rib side of the rack is a very fine, thin, gossamer-like skin coating the ribs. This must be removed before cooking or the ribs will be tough as old boots. It's very easy to remove – take a sharp knife and, from the top of the last rib bone, scrape the skin away from the cut bone end. It should come away easily. Once you have enough to pull away, get a piece of kitchen towel, grab hold of the skin and pull. It will tear away easily along the whole inside of the rib cage.

✱ Put the whole racks into a large pan, cover with water and add the stock cube. Bring to the boil, then cover with a lid, reduce the heat and simmer gently for 1–2 hours, or until the meat is almost falling off the bone, topping up the water if necessary.

✱ Remove from the heat and leave the racks to cool in the stock. Drain the ribs, pat dry and place in a large, resealable plastic food bag.

✱ Mix the marinade ingredients together thoroughly, reserve half and add the other half to the racks in the bag, coating the ribs well. Seal the bag and leave in the fridge for 2 hours, or preferably overnight.

✱ Preheat the oven to 190°C/Gas 5.

✱ Lay the racks, meaty-side up, on a sheet of foil in a shallow roasting dish and coat with the reserved marinade. Cover the ribs with a tent of foil and roast for about 45 minutes–1 hour, spooning over the marinade occasionally so that the ribs are nicely glazed, uncovering for the last 15 minutes of cooking.

✱ Remove the dish from the oven and leave the ribs to cool for 10–15 minutes before serving.

Barbecue spare ribs

BABY BACK RIBS ARE SO DELICIOUS, THEY HAVE TO BE IN THE BOOK. BE CAREFUL NOT TO OVERCOOK THEM, OTHERWISE THE MEAT WILL LITERALLY FALL OFF THE BONE. PREPARE AND COOK THESE IN THE SAME MANNER AS THE CHINESE-STYLE RIBS (LEFT). AS WITH ALL THE RIB RECIPES, THEY CAN BE FINISHED ON THE BARBECUE IN THE SUMMER MONTHS.

Serves 4   Preparation time 2 hours or overnight marinating, plus cooling
Cooking time 1–2 hours simmering, 45 minutes–1 hour roasting

1kg whole racks baby back pork ribs
10g beef stock cube, crumbled

MARINADE
1 tablespoon Dijon mustard
½ teaspoon smoked paprika
6 tablespoons tomato ketchup
4 tablespoons fresh lemon juice
4 tablespoons teriyaki sauce
4 tablespoons dark muscovado sugar
1 teaspoon Worcestershire sauce

Indian-style ribs

IT IS QUITE UNUSUAL TO SEE THESE RIBS, AS PORK IS NOT EATEN IN MUCH OF INDIA, BUT GOA IN THE WEST IS THE EXCEPTION, OWING TO ITS PORTUGUESE COLONIAL HERITAGE. THE MIX OF SPICES REALLY WORKS WELL, AND THE KETCHUP AND MANGO ADD A NICE SWEET EDGE TO THE WHOLE DISH. THIS AND THE OTHER RIB RECIPES ALL FREEZE BEAUTIFULLY. PREPARE AND COOK THESE IN THE SAME MANNER AS THE CHINESE-STYLE RIBS (LEFT).

Serves 4   Preparation time 2 hours or overnight marinating, plus cooling
Cooking time 1–2 hours simmering, 45 minutes–1 hour roasting

1kg whole racks pork ribs – baby back, loin or spare
10g beef stock cube, crumbled

MARINADE
6 tablespoons vegetable oil
6 tablespoons wine vinegar
6 tablespoons tomato ketchup
1 tablespoon mango chutney
1½ tablespoons finely grated fresh ginger
1 tablespoon grated garlic
1 tablespoon ground coriander
3 teaspoons cumin powder
1 teaspoon chilli powder

American-style pulled pork

FOR A SANDWICH, FORGET ROAST PORK – THIS IS WITHOUT QUESTION THE ONLY OPTION.

Serves 10–12   Preparation time 10 minutes   Cooking time 12 or 14 hours

1 pork butt or collar (cut from the neck of the pig), usually weighing about 2–2.5kg

SPICE RUB
2 tablespoons salt
2 tablespoons caster sugar
2 tablespoons brown sugar
2 tablespoons ground cumin
2 tablespoons freshly ground black pepper
1 tablespoon cayenne pepper
4 tablespoons paprika

THE PROPER METHOD

✱ Cover the meat with the spice rub, place in a vacuum cooking bag and vacuum seal. Place the bag in a sous-vide water bath or steam combination oven and cook for 12 hours at 80°C.

✱ After cooking, remove the pork from the bag and pull apart into bite-sized strips. Slather with the barbecue sauce (marinade) on page 35 and enjoy.

THE IMPROVISED METHOD

✱ Once you have covered the meat with the spice rub, wrap it tightly in foil or clingfilm and place on a roasting rack in a roasting tray with 1cm water in the bottom. Wrap the tray and meat package tightly in foil to create a kind of tent.

✱ Set your oven to its lowest temperature – 80–90°C if possible – and cook for 14 hours.

CHAPTER 2 Belly, loin & fillet

As with any four-legged animal, the middle rear of the pig is where you will find what chefs and butchers call the 'prime' cuts. Loins are cooked or cured whole; the rib end is cut into thick pork chops, and comes, if you're lucky, with a nice layer of fat and a little kidney (my father's favourite). The belly, now a staple in any good kitchen, is cooked or cured in a variety of ways to produce everything from pancetta to rillons, chunks of salted pork gently sautéed in their own fat. Fillet, seen as the best and priciest cut, is usually either roasted whole or turned into escalopes and sautéed. It needs careful attention, though, as it can dry out very quickly – it's worth remembering that lean pork has less fat per kilo than cottage cheese.

The belly, loin and fillet can also be made into what seems like an endless variety of cooked and cured products. Take, for instance, bacon, probably the world's most popular pork product. Whether you want to produce streaky (belly) or back (loin), the permutations are vast. The recipes here are some of Simon's favourites, though for my own Full English breakfast or in a sandwich or roll with a free-range egg I'd opt for green (unsmoked) streaky bacon any day of the week. Other preparations from the loin include lomo (see page 81), a Spanish speciality that is salt cured then air dried, and is delicious sliced and served at room temperature with a chilled glass of white wine – the sweet, rosy cured loin is perfectly offset by the creamy, salty fat. Lardo, or speck, is another Italian speciality that is popular around the world, and is made by removing the thick back fat from loins and then curing it in salt and also sometimes herbs and pepper. A while ago, I spent a long time working on and off in a factory in Italy. When we finished our day's work we would walk back to the hotel, stopping off for a quick glass. The bar owner would always offer a board of cured meats and cheese to nibble on. It could be a light Parma-ham style cured leg or a small selection of salami, but my favourite was speck – a 4cm-thick cured piece of creamy fat, sliced gossamer thin and served with a little cracked pepper, I remember the taste, texture and flavour even to this day. The curing recipes that follow are all very simple and I would encourage you to give them a go. – Phil

Simple pork & raisin terrine

A SIMPLE TERRINE LIKE THIS IS REALLY VERY EASY TO MAKE. MANY A TIME IN FRANCE I HAVE STOPPED FOR A LIGHT LUNCH OR SNACK, AND WHICHEVER REGION YOU ARE IN YOU WILL ALWAYS FIND A LOCAL TERRINE OR PÂTÉ OF SOME SORT. I HAVE FOUND THAT INTRODUCING A LITTLE REDUCED MEAT JUICE OR ALCOHOL ALWAYS BRINGS OUT A DEEPER FLAVOUR. BRANDY AND SHERRY ARE USED FAIRLY OFTEN, BUT HERE I'VE OPTED FOR MADEIRA. MOST COOK SHOPS NOW SELL THE CLASSIC TERRINE DISH (MINE IS 10 X 26CM AND 8CM DEEP), BUT ANY DEEP, LIDDED OVENPROOF DISH WILL DO.

Makes 1 terrine   Preparation time 30 minutes   Cooking time 1 hour 30–45 minutes

4 shallots, finely chopped
3 garlic cloves, finely chopped
100ml Madeira
2 tablespoons roughly chopped fresh thyme leaves
200ml well-reduced and well-flavoured pork or chicken stock
12 rindless dry-cured bacon rashers
750g rindless pork belly, cut into large cubes for mincing/chopping, or ready-minced
100g cured pork belly, pancetta or bacon offcuts, cut into small cubes
150g pork back fat, cut into small cubes
50g raisins, soaked in boiling water for 20 minutes and water gently squeezed out
salt and freshly ground black pepper
vegetable oil, for oiling

✱ Preheat the oven to 150°C/Gas 2. Put the shallots, garlic, Madeira, thyme and stock together into a saucepan and bring to the boil. Reduce the heat and simmer for 10–15 minutes until you have a thick gravy, then leave to cool.

✱ Line a lidded terrine dish with the bacon rashers, overlapping them slightly.

✱ Mince or roughly chop the pork belly cubes, if not already minced, and put in a large bowl. Add the cured pork, back fat, raisins and the cooled gravy and mix really well. Season with pepper and a little salt, taking into consideration the salt from the bacon in the mix and also lining the terrine.

✱ Pack the mixture into the terrine, making sure there are no air pockets. Fold the bacon over in a crisscross fashion. Lay a double-thickness piece of foil on a chopping board and lightly oil on one side. Place the oiled side onto the bacon, press down firmly and secure. Then place the lid on the terrine.

✱ Stand the terrine in a deep baking tray and half-fill with boiling water. You may need to top this up during the cooking period. Carefully place the tray in the oven and cook for 1 hour 20–30 minutes.

✱ To check if it's cooked, insert a skewer or small knife into the meat – the juices should run clear. When cooked, remove from the oven and lift out of the water, then place on a clean tray. Lift off the lid and you will see that the terrine has reduced slightly and come away from the sides of the dish. Wrap a piece of card the same size as the terrine in clingfilm and place on top of the foil.

✱ Leave to cool for 30 minutes, then place a bag of sugar or a couple of unopened cans on top of the card – this will press the terrine and make it easier to cut when cold. Chill well in the fridge, probably best overnight.

✱ The next day, place the terrine in a large bowl, fill with warm water around the outside of the terrine and leave for 5 minutes. This will release the jelly and allow you to remove the terrine from its dish by turning it upside down and helping it out a little.

✱ Slice and serve with buttered toasted seeded bread.

Juicy pork cutlets
with warm winter coleslaw

I LIKE THIS DISH PURELY BECAUSE OF THE AMAZING DIFFERENCE THE BRINE MAKES. YES, YOU ONLY NEED 20 MINUTES TO COMPLETELY CHANGE THE STRUCTURE OF THE MEAT AND IT WILL BE FULL OF FLAVOUR AND REALLY JUICY. WINTER COLESLAW IS ANOTHER LOVELY SALAD, AND IF YOU CAN LEAVE IT TO MARINATE, ALL THE BETTER, AS THE VEG WILL SOFTEN BUT STILL RETAIN A NICE CRUNCH.

Serves 4   Preparation time 35 minutes, including cooling/standing   Cooking time 10–15 minutes

4 boneless, rindless pork cutlets, 2cm thick
2 tablespoons olive oil

BRINE
30g caster sugar
15g salt
300ml water

SALAD
¼ white cabbage, very finely sliced
¼ red cabbage, very finely sliced
1 large carrot, peeled and very finely sliced
4 spring onions, very finely sliced on the diagonal
1 small bunch roughly chopped fresh coriander

DRESSING
3 tablespoons walnut oil
3 tablespoons sherry vinegar
2 tablespoons olive oil
2 teaspoons caster sugar
1 garlic clove, crushed to a paste
½ teaspoon salt
½ teaspoon ground white pepper
pinch of dried chilli flakes with seeds

✱ Put the brine ingredients into a stainless steel saucepan. Dissolve the sugar and salt slowly in the water over a low heat, then bring to the boil. Remove from the heat and leave to cool, then top up with cold water to the original quantity of brine (345ml).

✱ Place the pork cutlets in a glass, ceramic or stainless steel bowl. Pour over the cold brine and mix well, then leave to stand in a cool place for 20–30 minutes.

✱ Meanwhile, prepare the salad ingredients. I find the best way is to finely slice the root vegetables using a food-processor fitted with a fine slicer attachment. Put the sliced vegetables in a bowl with the coriander.

✱ Combine all the dressing ingredients in a bowl and mix well. Transfer to a saucepan and gently warm; do not boil. Pour over the salad and mix really well, then leave in a warm place to marinate.

✱ Heat the olive oil in a frying pan. Drain the pork well, then pat dry with kitchen paper. Pan-fry gently for 3–4 minutes on each side. Serve with the warm coleslaw and a few boiled new potatoes.

COOKING IN A WOOD-FIRED OVEN

There is no set recipe to cooking in a wood-fired oven, as much depends on what type of oven you have, so what follows is a list of general points and advice. My own oven is wood-fired, though gas is also good and far more controllable.

LOGS Different woods burn for different times and, most importantly, at different heat levels. If seasoned correctly, cherry, oak, beech, etc, will all burn at roughly the same heat and for the same length of time, so these are what I use. I steer clear of resin woods such as pine as they impart an awful flavour and smoke. Green (freshly cut) wood is difficult to burn as it's full of sap. The only time I use a little green wood is if I want to produce a bit more of a smoke flavour. So all wood must be seasoned or dried correctly. I use a redundant greenhouse for drying my wood. I cut in the late winter, split any green, then store all the spring and summer so it dries perfectly. I normally work a year ahead of myself so I can cook all year round. I then split my logs into 50cm lengths, say 30-40cm across, as I find these burn well and evenly for my oven, giving a constant heat, though I use chunkier logs if I want a lot more heat for steaks or pizzas.

LIGHTING THE FIRE I use small bundles of kindling and paper to get the fire going (never firelighters or lighting fluid) then thinner pieces of wood, the same length, to keep the fire at a constant temperature, for when cooking larger pieces of meat or whole suckling pigs (see below). When the embers are red-hot they only need a few bits of wood to keep them going. I light my fire roughly 45 minutes to an hour in advance so the oven reaches the right heat and is stable. My builder, Paul, told me that once the flue and bricks are warm, the smoke will disappear, and generally speaking it does, so don't be too worried about smoke at the start. Another reason to wait for the oven to warm up.

COOKING I tend to move my fire around every time I cook, but have found that cooking to one side tends to be a good starting point. Once the oven is warm, you need small amounts of thinner wood to keep the temperature constant, the most important part of wood-fired oven cooking. Making the fire at the rear of the oven is good for larger cuts or joints of meat that need to be cooked for longer as this means they can be positioned away from the heat. If I'm cooking pizzas, steaks, chops or cutlets I make the fire slap bang in the middle, then once the oven has reached the required heat I push the embers to the rear of the oven and bake on the very hot stones.

EQUIPMENT I use a large wire brush for brushing away hot embers, plus a couple of homemade pokers and rectangular trays for catching fatty deposits when roasting meat. Probably the most important of all, though, is a laser thermometer – brilliant for checking the temperature all round the oven and also of the food you are cooking

That's pretty much it. It's a bit like learning to fly fish, it takes a day to learn, but a lifetime to master. It's all a matter of practice and seeing what works for you. The best piece of advice is to keep checking the temperature and the fire.

Suckling pig

I TEND TO USE A SMALLER PIG, 8-10KG. I DON'T SCORE THE FLESH, JUST SEASON IT WELL, BOTH INSIDE AND OUT, THEN PLACE ON A TRAY TO CATCH ALL THE JUICES. DURING COOKING, MOVE THE TRAY AROUND AND ALSO TURN THE PIG AND BASTE AT REGULAR INTERVALS TO ENSURE AN EVEN COOK. THE IMPORTANT THING IS TO KEEP A CAREFUL EYE ON THE PIG AND TO COOK IT LONG AND SLOW. IF YOU DO SO, YOU REALLY CAN'T GO WRONG.

Flash-fried pork skirt with cucumber, tomato & chilli pickle

THE SKIRT STEAK ON A PIG IS SIMILAR TO THE BAVETTE ON A BEEF CARCASS. IT'S A DELICATE CUT FROM INSIDE THE LEG THAT GETS LARGELY FORGOTTEN. IT'S SO TENDER, LEAN AND JUICY THAT THE LESS YOU DO WITH IT, THE BETTER, IN MY VIEW. YOU CAN FLASH-FRY IT, AS I DO IN THIS RECIPE, OR SIMPLY GRILL, BUT YOU MUST MAKE SURE YOU DO NOT OVERCOOK IT. THE BEST THING TO DO IS TO HALF COOK IT, MAKING NOTE OF HOW LONG YOU DID SO, THEN REMOVE FROM IT THE HEAT SOURCE, LIGHTLY COVER WITH A PIECE OF FOIL AND LEAVE TO REST FOR THE EXACT SAME TIME. IT WILL BE COOKED TO PERFECTION. NEITHER OVERCOOKED, OR UNDERCOOKED JUST PERFECT! HERE I SERVE IT WITH A CRUNCHY, SHARP CUCUMBER AND TOMATO SALAD, MARINATED WITH A LITTLE CHILLI.

Serves 4   Preparation time 20 minutes   Cooking time 6–8 minutes maximum

150ml rice wine vinegar
1 large cucumber, finely chopped
4 ripe tomatoes, finely chopped
4 small spring onions, finely chopped
6 tablespoons olive oil
pinch sugar
4 x 125–150g pieces of pork skirt
1 tablespoon unsalted butter
75g baby spinach leaves
salt and freshly ground black pepper

✱ Bring the rice vinegar to the boil, simmer for 3-4 minutes, then cool.

✱ Place the cucumber, tomatoes, spring onion and 4 tablespoons olive oil in a bowl, season with a pinch of black pepper, then add the sugar and vinegar and leave for 20 minutes.

✱ Heat a large frying pan and add the remaining olive oil. Season the skirts really well, add to the hot oil and cook for 3-4 minutes. Turn over, add the butter and cook for a further 2-3 minutes, basting with the oil and the nut brown butter.

✱ Remove from the pan, loosely cover with foil and leave to rest in a warm place for 6–7 minutes.

✱ Just before serving, add the spinach leaves to the cucumber and tomato mixture and allow them to wilt slightly.

✱ Pile the salad onto 4 plates and top with the skirt steak. It's as simple as that. If you want to be a bit cheffy, you can cut the skirt across the grain of the meat into 5 or 6 slices.

Porchetta

TRADITIONALLY, PORCHETTA IS A BONELESS SUCKLING PIG SEASONED WITH SALT, HERBS AND SPICES AND ROASTED IN A WOOD-FIRED OVEN. MY VERSION USES JUST THE MIDDLE OF THE ANIMAL, THE LOIN AND BELLY.

Makes 1kg   Preparation time 10 minutes   Cooking time 40 minutes, plus 40 minutes resting

1kg boneless pork (from the middle)

SPICE RUB
1 tablespoon salt
1 tablespoon fennel seeds, crushed
1 teaspoon coarsely ground black pepper
1 teaspoon dried thyme
1 teaspoon smoked paprika
4 garlic cloves, chopped

✱ Mix all the spice rub ingredients together thoroughly and rub into the meat. Preheat the oven to 200°C/Gas 6.

✱ Roll the belly part into the thicker loin part and tie securely. Then score finely with a sharp knife. Roast in the oven for 40 minutes, then remove and leave to rest for a further 40 minutes before serving.

Rillettes

PERHAPS ONE OF THE MOST DECADENT THINGS YOU CAN EAT (WELL I THINK SO ANYWAY), RILLETTES IS SIMILAR TO A PÂTÉ IN THAT YOU CAN SPREAD IT ON BREAD OR TOAST. SINCE IT IS PRESERVED IN THE FAT IT'S COOKED IN, IT ISN'T FOR THE FAINT-HEARTED.

Makes 1kg   Preparation time 10 minutes, plus standing   Cooking time 4–5 hours

1kg pork collar, cut into strips
200g pork back fat, cut into small cubes
20g cooking salt
3g ground white pepper
3 garlic cloves, chopped
1 tablespoon chopped fresh thyme

✱ Mix the meat and fat with all the seasonings in a large bowl, then cover and leave to stand overnight in the fridge.

✱ Preheat the oven to 140°C/Gas 1.

✱ Pack the meat mixture into a terrine dish or deep, lidded ovenproof dish, cover with the lid and cook for 4–5 hours until the meat is fork tender.

✱ Once it is cooked, remove the meat from the dish, reserving the fat, and shred with a fork. Press the shredded pork into the cleaned dish.

✱ Put the reserved fat into a pan and gently melt, then pour a thin layer over the rillettes. Chill overnight and enjoy.

Crisp, succulent pork belly with gherkin & shallot dressing

PORK BELLY IS ALL THE RAGE THESE DAYS, PARTLY BECAUSE IT'S CHEAP, EASY TO COOK AND YOU REALLY HAVE TO GO TO SOME EFFORT TO MESS IT UP. HOWEVER, IT CAN BE A BIT FATTY AND THIS CAN PUT A LOT OF PEOPLE OFF. ONE OF THE BEST WAYS OF AVOIDING THIS IS TO MAKE SURE THE SKIN IS CRISP. HERE IS A SUCCULENT RECIPE, WITH A SHARP RELISH/MAYO TO CUT THE RICHNESS.

Serves 4   Preparation time 25 minutes, plus 12 hours or overnight standing and then chilling
Cooking time about 2 hours 20 minutes

55g salt
1.5kg piece of boneless pork belly, rind on
6 garlic cloves, very well crushed
a few sprigs of fresh thyme
about 800ml sunflower oil

DRESSING
8 heaped tablespoons mayonnaise
6 large gherkins, finely chopped
½ turnip, peeled and very finely chopped
3 large shallots, very finely chopped
4 tablespoons chopped fresh flat-leaf parsley
juice of ½ lemon, or to taste
½ teaspoon freshly ground black pepper

✱ Rub the salt over the pork, then rub the garlic and thyme in well. Place the pork in a glass dish, cover with clingfilm and leave to stand in the fridge for 12 hours or overnight.

✱ The following day, preheat the oven to 160°C/Gas 3. Remove the clingfilm, wash the salt, garlic and thyme off the pork, pat dry, then place in a small, deep roasting tray just large enough to fit the pork.

✱ Gently heat the sunflower oil and carefully pour over the pork so that it is submerged. Cover with foil and carefully place the tray in the oven to cook for about 2 hours, or until a knife can pass through the pork easily. The meat should be very soft and almost too difficult to pick up, but not stringy and overcooked. Remove from the oven and leave to cool.

✱ Lift out the pork, place on a flat tray, rind-side down, and cover with clingfilm. Press down another tray on top and then chill well.

✱ When ready to cook, preheat the oven to 220°C/Gas 7.

✱ Cut the pork into four perfect squares and trim off any ragged edges.

✱ Heat a dry non-stick ovenproof frying pan on the hob, place the pork rind-side down in the pan and cook until the skin begins to crackle.

✱ Transfer to the oven and cook for 15 minutes.

✱ Meanwhile, for the dressing, put the mayo, gherkins, turnip, shallots and parsley in a bowl and mix really well. Add lemon juice to taste and the black pepper.

✱ Serve the pork, crispy-side up, with some small florets of broccoli and the dressing.

Juicy pork chops with strawberries & mustard

ALTHOUGH THIS COMBINATION SOUNDS A LITTLE BIZARRE, IT COMES FROM A VERY OLD ENGLISH RECIPE AND IS DELICIOUS, I PROMISE. THE ACID IN THE STRAWBERRY MARINADE BREAKS DOWN THE STRUCTURE OF THE MEAT VERY WELL INDEED, SIMILAR TO THE REACTION OF MARINATING MEAT IN YOGURT, INDIAN STYLE. IT ALSO UTILISES THOSE VERY SOFT STRAWBERRIES LEFT OVER IN THE BOTTOM OF THE PUNNET.

Serves 4   Preparation time 20 minutes, plus marinating/cooling   Cooking time 20–25 minutes

4 thick pork chops or cutlets
2 tablespoons olive oil
salt and freshly ground black pepper

MARINADE
250g ripe, tasty English strawberries
75ml olive oil
juice of 2 large lemons
2 tablespoons white wine vinegar
1 tablespoon strawberry jam or other jam
2 teaspoons Dijon mustard
1 small onion, finely chopped
2 garlic cloves, chopped

✷ For the marinade, wash the strawberries well, then put 200g into a blender, reserving the rest for later. Add all the remaining marinade ingredients with salt and pepper and blitz until smooth.

✷ Strain the purée well to remove the seeds, then adjust the seasoning if necessary.

✷ Using a sharp knife, nick the fat and the rind of each chop or cutlet, then pierce the meat lightly. Place in a glass or ceramic dish and pour over half the strawberry marinade. Cover and leave to marinate for 20 minutes at room temperature, or longer in the fridge, but overnight at most.

✷ Put the remaining marinade in a saucepan and cook for 10 minutes – it will thicken up nicely. Leave to cool.

✷ When ready to cook, preheat the oven to 200°C/Gas 6.

✷ Warm a large ovenproof frying pan on the hob and add the olive oil. Remove the chops or cutlets from their marinade and pat dry with kitchen paper, then season well with salt and pepper. Add to the warm oil and cook for about 4–5 minutes until lightly browned on the underside.

✷ Turn over, pop into the oven and cook for 6–8 minutes until cooked through; do not overcook.

✷ Remove from the oven and cover with foil, then leave for 10 minutes to relax.

✷ Chop the reserved strawberries and add to the cooled marinade to make a relish. Serve the pork chops or cutlets with the relish and the Quinoa, Rice & Salted Cashew Salad (see opposite).

Quinoa, rice & salted cashew salad

A NICE NUTTY SALAD THAT WORKS PERFECTLY WITH PORK CHOPS, OR INDEED ANY ROASTED OR GRILLED MEATS. THE KEY THING HERE IS TO NOT OVERCOOK THE QUINOA SO THAT YOU KEEP ITS CRUNCHY EDGE.

Serves 4   Preparation time 10 minutes   Cooking time 15–20 minutes

150g quinoa
200g cooked basmati rice
1 small bag watercress
1 small bag rocket
100g salted honeyed cashews, chopped
salt and freshly ground black pepper

DRESSING
5 tablespoons olive oil
juice of 2 large limes
juice of 1 orange
1 garlic clove, crushed
1 large red onion, finely sliced

✱ Put the quinoa into a saucepan and cover well with cold water. Bring to the boil, then reduce the heat and simmer gently for about 15 minutes, or until just tender but nice and nutty; do not overcook. Strain well and tip into a bowl, then add the cooked rice and mix well.

✱ For the dressing, combine the olive oil and lime and orange juices in a separate bowl, then add the garlic and sliced onion and mix well.

✱ Roughly chop the watercress and rocket, then add to the quinoa and rice along with the cashews.

✱ Add the dressing, season well with salt and pepper and mix well. Serve with the Juicy Pork Chops with Strawberries & Mustard (see opposite).

Grilled pork chops with baked pears

BRINING IS NOTHING NEW. IN FACT, IT'S BEEN AROUND FOR CENTURIES – TAKE DELICIOUS BACON, FOR EXAMPLE. THE SECRET OF SUCCESS IS TO BRINE ONLY LIGHTLY, AS WITH THESE CHOPS, WHICH REQUIRE 20 MINUTES MAXIMUM – YES, JUST 20 MINUTES. AS THEY SAY, JUST TASTE THE DIFFERENCE...

Serves 4   Preparation time 20 minutes   Cooking time 2 hours

4 thick, nice and fatty pork chops, 2–2.5cm thick
2 tablespoons olive oil

BRINE
30g caster sugar
15g salt
300ml water

PEARS
4 large ripe Conference pears
8 tablespoons maple syrup
8 tablespoons olive oil
salt and freshly ground black pepper

✱ Preheat the oven to 160°C/Gas 3.

✱ Cut the pears in half lengthways, then cut a small sliver off the bottom of each so they sit nicely level, and scoop out the core and pips with spoon. Put the pears on a baking tray.

✱ Drizzle over the maple syrup and olive oil, and season with a touch of salt and pepper. Bake for about 2 hours, or until soft. The pears will shrivel and brown slightly, but the flavour will intensify by about threefold.

✱ Meanwhile, put the brine ingredients into a stainless steel saucepan. Dissolve the sugar and salt slowly into the water over a low heat, then bring to the boil. Remove from the heat and leave to cool, then top up with cold water to the original quantity of brine (345ml).

✱ Pour half the brine into a small glass, ceramic or stainless steel tray. Place the chops in the tray so that they fit nice and snugly. Pour over the remainder of the brine. Cover and leave to stand at room temperature for 20 minutes, no more.

✱ When you are ready to cook, remove the chops from the brine and pat dry with kitchen paper. Heat the olive oil in a frying pan. Lightly pepper the chops, then cook gently for 4–5 minutes on each side until cooked through.

✱ Arrange the baked pears roughly sliced topping the chops. Serve with some lightly cooked green beans.

Cider pot-roasted pork belly with apples & celery

YOU REALLY CAN'T GO WRONG WITH ANY DISH THAT MATCHES CIDER WITH PORK. IT IS SUCH A CLASSIC COMBINATION IN COOKING, AND ONE THAT HARKS BACK TO THE CUSTOM MANY YEARS AGO FOR PIGS TO BE LET OUT TO GORGE ON THE FALLEN APPLES IN ORDER TO CLEAR THE ORCHARDS. BELLY IS PERFECT FOR THIS SORT OF COOKING – NOT TOO FATTY, AND THIN ENOUGH TO POT ROAST QUICKLY AND EVENLY. POT-ROASTING IN A SMALL AMOUNT OF LIQUID IN AN ENCLOSED PAN IS BRILLIANT. YOU WILL BE AMAZED HOW MUCH STOCK THERE WILL BE AT THE END, MAKING A GREAT SAUCE/COMPOTE.

Serves 4   Preparation time 30 minutes   Cooking time about 2 hours in total, probably less

650g piece of boneless, rindless pork belly
2 tablespoons oil (any type will do)
100g chorizo or any spicy sausage, roughly chopped (optional)
4 large celery sticks, finely chopped
2 large onions, very finely chopped
1 large Bramley apple, peeled, cored and finely chopped
6 garlic cloves, finely chopped
a few fresh sage leaves
1 small glass dry cider
1 small glass well-flavoured pork or chicken stock
salt and freshly ground black pepper

✷ Preheat the oven to 180°C/Gas 4.

✷ Season the pork belly well with salt and pepper. Heat the oil in a deep, ovenproof pan with a tight-fitting lid on the hob, add the chorizo, if using, and cook until the fat starts to run.

✷ Add the pork belly and brown well on both sides, then carefully remove from the pan, leaving the chorizo.

✷ Add the vegetables, apple, garlic and sage to the pan and top with the pork, then pour in the cider and stock. Bring to the boil and cover with the lid.

✷ Cook in the oven for 1 hour and 30–45 minutes, or until the pork is soft and well cooked – but do not overcook!

✷ Remove the pork from the pan and carefully chop or slice. Gently mash the veg and apples with the gravy and juices in the pan and cook on the hob until thickened slightly. Serve with the pork.

Roast loin of pork with crackling & apple sauce

THERE ARE TWO KEY ISSUES HERE: ONE, SCORE THE RIND AND FAT REALLY WELL, AS THIS WILL ENSURE THAT THE FAT WILL BE RELEASED, MAKING A CRISPER CRACKLING; TWO, DO NOT OVERCOOK AND BE CERTAIN TO REST THE PORK, WELL WRAPPED IN FOIL. I ALWAYS SAY TO REST MEAT FOR AS LONG AS YOU COOK IT. YES, THAT'S AN HOUR IN THIS CASE, BUT IT WILL BE FINE, TRUST ME – JUST POP IT BACK IN THE OVEN TO WARM UP AGAIN.

Serves 6-8   Preparation time 15 minutes   Cooking time 1 hour 15-45 minutes

1.5kg boneless rolled loin of pork, rind scored with a Stanley knife
salt and freshly ground black pepper
1 tablespoon plain flour
300ml hot chicken or pork stock

APPLE SAUCE
½ teaspoon ground allspice
about 200ml cold water
3 large, tart cooking apples, such as Bramleys, peeled, cored and chopped
50g unsalted butter

* Preheat the oven to 190°C/Gas 5.

* Rip off about a 50cm length of foil from the roll, scrunch up into a small bed for the pork to sit on – this is to stop the bottom of the pork frying in its own fat and juices – and place in a roasting tray. Season the pork rind well with salt and pepper, sit the pork on the scrunched-up foil and pop the pork in the oven. Roast for 1 hour.

* For the apple sauce, put the spice, water and apples in a saucepan, cover with a lid and cook for 15 minutes until the apples are soft and pulpy and you have a nice thick stew. Season with a little salt and pepper and stir in the butter. Keep warm.

* After 1 hour, remove the pork from the oven and check that it is cooked by inserting a skewer or thin-bladed knife into the thickest part of the meat – the juices should run clear. If not, return to the oven for a further 15–30 minutes.

* Remove the pork rind with a long-bladed knife, ensuring that you keep most of the fat on the loin. Place the rind on a baking tray, fat-side up, and pop back in the oven for about 15–20 minutes to crisp up further, but take care as the crackling will quickly burn.

* Meanwhile, wrap the pork well in foil and leave to rest in a warm place, to let the juices settle and the meat tenderise.

* Place the roasting tray on the hob and scrape off all the bits stuck to the bottom. Mix the flour with a little water in a cup. Spoon off a little of the fat, then add the flour and water mixture and stir well to soak up the remaining fat. Blend in the hot stock and cook, stirring well, until thickened, then pour into a jug and keep warm.

* Cut the pork into thick slices and serve topped with pieces of the crisp crackling, with the warm apple sauce on the side.

Pork fillet escalopes with blackcurrants & double cream

FRESH BLACKCURRANTS ARE ONLY AROUND FOR A COUPLE OF MONTHS, SO IT'S BEST TO MAKE THE MOST OF THEM. THEIR TANGY EDGE REALLY HELPS BRING OUT THE FLAVOUR OF PORK AND CREAM, BUT I HAVE FOUND THAT FROZEN AND EVEN CANNED BLACKCURRANTS ARE PRETTY GOOD FOR THIS DISH. I BUY PLENTY OF FRESH BLACKCURRANTS IN THE SUMMER AND THEN FREEZE THEM, AS THEY ARE GREAT FOR SPICING UP STEWS AND BRAISES IN THE WINTER MONTHS.

Serves 4   Preparation time 30 minutes, plus chilling   Cooking time 25 minutes

1 pork fillet, about 500g, without fat or silver sinew
3 eggs
1 tablespoon milk
5 tablespoons vegetable oil
4 tablespoons plain flour
6 tablespoons dried breadcrumbs
6 tablespoons cornmeal (fine polenta)
1 small onion, finely chopped
1 garlic clove, crushed
200ml dry white wine
275ml good-quality chicken stock
100g fresh blackcurrants (frozen are also fine, or use canned)
150ml double cream
squeeze of lemon juice
salt and freshly ground black pepper

✱ Place the pork on a chopping board and cut into four pieces, then cut each piece of pork three-quarters of the way through lengthways and open out flat.

✱ Lay a large piece of clingfilm over a chopping board. Place one piece of pork on the clingfilm, add ½ teaspoon water and fold the clingfilm over. Using a rolling pin or meat mallet, gently beat the pork nice and thin, the thinner the better. (The water helps the pork to move inside the clingfilm.) Repeat the process with the other three pieces of pork.

✱ Put the eggs, milk and 1 tablespoon vegetable oil into a bowl and beat together well. Put the flour into one dish and combine the breadcrumbs and cornmeal in another. Dust the pork lightly with flour, then dip, one at a time, into the egg mixture then into the breadcrumbs and cornmeal. Chill well.

✱ Meanwhile, place the onion and garlic in a saucepan, add the white wine and bring to the boil. Reduce the heat and simmer until about 1 tablespoon remains.

✱ Add the stock and cook down until you have about half the original volume. Add the blackcurrants (if fresh) and cook for 3–4 minutes. (If using frozen fruit, pop them in straight from the freezer and cook for 5–6 minutes.)

✱ Add the cream and bring to the boil, but do not reduce. Season well and taste, adjusting with a little sugar if needed and a squeeze of lemon juice. If you are using canned blackcurrants, add them now so that the residual heat warms them through, then cover.

✱ Heat the remaining vegetable oil in a frying pan, add two pork escalopes and cook quickly in the hot oil until slightly browned on the base. Turn over and cook for further 3–4 minutes. Remove from the pan, drain well and keep warm while you repeat the process with the remaining escalopes.

✱ To serve, spoon a little sauce onto each warmed plate and top with a hot pork escalope. Serve the extra sauce separately. All you will need with it is a crisp green salad a few new potatoes rolled in minted butter.

Bonfire spiced pork & prune patties

THIS IS A QUICK AND EASY DISH TO MAKE, AND ADDING PRUNES TO THE PORK REALLY SWEETENS THE MEAT NICELY. I LIKE TO COOK THESE PATTIES ON AN OPEN FIRE.

Serves 4   Preparation time 20 minutes   Cooking time about 10 minutes

6 ready-to-eat pitted prunes
450g lean minced pork
2 tablespoons chopped fresh sage
¼ teaspoon ground nutmeg
2 pinches of chilli powder
1 tablespoon mayonnaise
1 egg, lightly beaten
2 tablespoons vegetable oil
salt and freshly ground black pepper

SAUCE
225ml tomato ketchup
125ml cold water
2 tablespoons Worcestershire sauce
55g soft light brown sugar
25g runny honey
3 tablespoons malt vinegar
2 teaspoons English mustard powder
1 teaspoon Cajun seasoning
1 teaspoon ground cumin
2 pinches of chopped fresh chilli

✱ Put all the sauce ingredients into a saucepan and bring to the boil. Reduce the heat and simmer gently for 2 minutes, or until slightly thickened. Season with salt and pepper. Keep hot or leave to cool ready for serving.

✱ Chop the prunes into small pieces and put in a bowl. Add the minced pork, sage, nutmeg, chilli powder and mayonnaise and season really well with salt and pepper. Then mix in a little of the beaten egg to bind everything together.

✱ Mould the mixture into eight small flat patties. Alternatively, you can mould the mixture onto small bamboo kebab skewers, presoaked in cold water for 30 minutes. They can be cooked in the same way as the patties.

✱ Heat the oil in a large non-stick frying pan and cook the patties (or kebabs) on each side for about 4–5 minutes. Serve straight away with the hot or cooled sauce.

Velveted pork fillet with peppers & garlic

PORK FILLET, I HAVE FOUND, CAN COOK UP RATHER BLAND, DRY AND TASTELESS. MY GOOD FRIEND KEN HOM SHOWED ME THIS TRICK MANY YEARS AGO, SO THANKS KEN! VELVETING IS A SIMPLE PROCESS IN WHICH YOU COAT MEAT OR FISH IN A MIXTURE OF BEATEN EGG WHITE, A LITTLE OIL, A PINCH OF SALT AND CORNFLOUR. THIS MIXTURE THEN CLINGS TO THE MEAT OR FISH AND, ONCE COOKED, SEALS IN ANY MOISTURE, MAKING THE END DISH BEAUTIFULLY TENDER AND MOIST.

Serves 4   Preparation time 10 minutes   Cooking time 15 minutes

1 egg white
1 tablespoon cornflour
1 pork fillet, about 500g, without fat or silver sinew, cut into 8–12 slices
1 red pepper, deseeded and cut into strips
1 yellow pepper, deseeded and cut into strips
1 onion, very finely sliced
4 tablespoons vegetable oil
2 garlic cloves, finely chopped
8 spring onions, or 1 small bunch, finely sliced
6 tablespoons dark soy sauce
salt

✱ Put the egg white and cornflour in a bowl with a pinch of salt, whisk together briefly, then fold through the pork slices until evenly coated.

✱ Put the peppers and onion in a saucepan with a pinch of salt, cover with water and bring to the boil, then immediately drain and leave to cool.

✱ Heat a wok or non-stick frying pan with 2 tablespoons of the vegetable oil. Add half the pork slices and stir-fry until nicely coloured, then remove from the pan to a plate. Repeat with the remaining pork until it is all sealed and then keep warm.

✱ Wipe out the pan with kitchen paper and reheat with the remaining 2 tablespoons oil. Add the cooled peppers and onion, garlic and spring onions and stir-fry over a high heat for 3–4 minutes, or until softened and coloured.

✱ Return the pork to the pan, add the soy sauce and stir well, then stir in any pork juice left over on the plate before serving with boiled or steamed plain rice or rice noodles.

Pork fillet with black peppercorns, vinegar & yellow bean sauce

THIS IS A GREAT WAY TO EAT PORK FILLET, BUT TAKE CARE NOT TO OVERCOOK IT, OR THE MEAT WILL BE DRY AND TOUGH. I HAVE NO PROBLEM USING A SHOP-BOUGHT SAUCE IN THIS INSTANCE, ESPECIALLY AS SOME OF THEM ARE SUCH GOOD QUALITY.

Serves 4   Preparation time 10 minutes   Cooking time 25 minutes

1 pork fillet, about 500g, without fat and silver sinew, cut into 8 slices
2 tablespoons olive oil
30g unsalted butter
2 tablespoons plain flour
1 teaspoon lightly crushed black peppercorns
2 tablespoons white wine vinegar
3 tablespoons good-quality Chinese yellow bean sauce
200ml double cream
6 tablespoons roughly chopped fresh flat-leaf parsley
caster sugar, to taste
salt

✱ Flatten each slice of pork fillet with the blade of a knife so that you end up with eight small escalopes.

✱ Heat the olive oil and butter in a non-stick frying pan. Season the escalopes with a little salt, then gently dust with flour, shaking off the excess. Place four escalopes into the hot oil and melted butter and cook over a medium heat for 3–4 minutes each side – they should be nicely browned and golden. Remove from the pan and keep warm, then repeat with the remaining escalopes.

✱ Add the crushed peppercorns and vinegar and swill around the pan – the vinegar will mostly evaporate – then add the yellow bean sauce and heat through. Stir in the cream and bring to the boil, then add the parsley. Season with a little sugar, and salt if needed.

✱ Return all the pork to the pan, spoon over the sauce and serve with boiled or steamed plain rice.

Pumpkin & pork hot pot

THE TRADITIONAL WAY OF MAKING HOT POT IS TO CASSEROLE SCRAG END OF LAMB WITH A POTATO CRUST PACKED FULL OF ROOT VEGETABLES. IN THIS VERSION I HAVE ADDED BLACK PUDDING AND PUMPKIN, THE LATTER REPLACING THE USUAL SWEDE AND TURNIP AND THE FORMER GIVING THE WHOLE DISH A PEPPERY BITE, AND HAVE USED PORK NECK CHOPS INSTEAD OF LAMB, AS THEY HAVE A LITTLE MORE MEAT ON THEM AND SLIGHTLY LESS FAT. YOU CAN ALSO ADD SOAKED PEARL BARLEY IF YOU WISH. MY MUM STILL MAKES THE BEST HOT POT.

Serves 4   Preparation time 20 minutes   Cooking time about 2 hours

4–6 tablespoons vegetable oil
1 large carrot, peeled and chopped
2 small onions, roughly chopped
2 large garlic cloves, crushed
4 pork neck chops or thick pork chops
280g peeled and deseeded pumpkin, diced
115g good-quality black pudding, sliced on the diagonal
10g beef stock cube, dissolved in about 600ml boiling water
2 tablespoons plain flour
4 large baking potatoes, peeled and not-too-thinly sliced
melted butter, for brushing
salt and freshly ground black pepper

✱ Preheat the oven to 180°C/Gas 4.

✱ Heat half the oil in a sauté pan and cook the carrot, onions and garlic together until they have wilted and taken on a nice colour.

✱ Heat the remaining oil in a frying pan and cook the chops until nicely browned on both sides, then transfer to a roasting tray or ovenproof dish with a tight-fitting lid.

✱ Spread the pumpkin and the cooked vegetable mixture over the chops and season well with salt and pepper, then top with the black pudding slices.

✱ Blend the warm stock into the flour, then pour over the chops to just cover them. Carefully top with the sliced potatoes, season well with salt and pepper and brush with melted butter.

✱ Cover with foil or the lid and cook in the oven for about 1 hour. Remove the foil and return the pan or dish to the oven for a further 45 minutes–1 hour to brown up the potatoes. You may need to increase the oven temperature to crisp them up.

✱ This dish is best cooked and eaten when it has been left to cool for about 30 minutes. I'm a great fan of pickled cabbage and it works perfectly with hot pot, so just tuck in.

My Pho

HAVING BEEN TO VIETNAM RECENTLY, IT MADE SENSE TO INCLUDE MY VERSION OF THE COUNTRY'S NATIONAL DISH, PHO, PRONOUNCED 'FIR' IN VIETNAMESE. I HAD A BEEF PHO FOR BREAKFAST, EATEN ON THE SIDE OF THE STREET VERY EARLY ONE MORNING. THE FRESHNESS OF THE DISH REALLY MADE AN IMPACT ON ME, WITH ITS TASTY, CLEAN FLAVOURS ALL WORKING WELL TOGETHER. IT IS ALSO GLUTEN FREE, SOMETHING THAT IS CLOSE TO MY HEART. THERE ARE MANY VARIATIONS OF PHO TO BE FOUND IN VIETNAM FROM NORTH TO SOUTH, USING CHICKEN OR FISH AS WELL AS BEEF. ONE IS EVEN SERVED WITH SLICED BREAD FOR DUNKING.

Serves 4   Preparation time 20 minutes   Cooking time 15 minutes

1 litre good-quality chicken or pork stock
  or use 1 litre water and 3–4 x 10g chicken or pork stock cubes, crumbled
8 spring onions, sliced on the diagonal
1 small fresh red chilli, finely chopped
2 garlic cloves, crushed
2 tablespoons Vietnamese fish sauce (nuoc cham)
1 tablespoon palm sugar or caster sugar
1 small pork fillet, about 350g, without fat or silver sinew
200g cooked rice vermicelli or other fine rice noodles
200g beansprouts
1 small bunch fresh coriander
1 small bunch fresh Thai basil or any other basil
10 fresh mint leaves
juice of 2 large limes
salt and freshly ground black pepper

✱ Put the stock or water and stock cubes into a large saucepan and heat until just simmering.

✱ Add the spring onions, chilli, garlic, fish sauce, sugar and a little salt and pepper.

✱ Meanwhile, cut the pork into very thin slices across the fillet, then into four.

✱ Add the pork to the stock and stir well – it will cook almost straight away.

✱ Add the noodles and beansprouts, return to a simmer and then turn off the heat.

✱ Roughly chop the herbs and add to the pan along with the lime juice. Serve straight away. You can serve a little soy sauce with the pho if you want, along with extra limes for squeezing, herbs and even more chilli.

Pork fillet jalfrezi

CHICKEN IS THE NORM FOR JALFREZI, WHICH ORIGINATED AS A USE-UP DISH IN THE DAYS OF THE RAJ. THE WELL-TO-DO FAMILIES IN DELHI ALWAYS HAD A ROAST ON A SUNDAY, AND ANY LEFTOVER ROASTED MEAT WAS REUSED ON MONDAY IN A SORT OF STIR-FRY. I ENJOYED A PARTICULARLY DELICIOUS JALFREZI COOKED BY THE CHEF OF THE OBEROI HOTEL IN NEW DELHI, SO HERE IS THE PRODUCT OF WHAT I LEARNED FROM THAT EXPERIENCE.

Serves 4   Preparation time 30 minutes   Cooking time 15 minutes

400g can chopped tomatoes in juice
½ x 10g vegetable stock cube, crumbled
1 tablespoon tomato purée
4 tablespoons vegetable oil
2 small pork fillets, 300–350g each, or 1 large, about 500g,
    without fat and silver sinew, cut into 12 pieces
1 tablespoon very finely chopped fresh ginger
1 garlic clove, finely chopped
1–2 teaspoons roughly chopped fresh red chilli
1 teaspoon ground cumin
1 teaspoon ground coriander
½ teaspoon ground turmeric
1 small onion, very finely chopped
1 small red pepper, deseeded and sliced
1 small yellow pepper, deseeded and sliced
1 small green pepper, deseeded and sliced
caster sugar, to taste
2 tablespoons chopped fresh coriander
salt and freshly ground black pepper

* Put the tomatoes, stock cube and tomato purée in a saucepan and cook down until you have a thick stew.

* Heat half the oil in a large pan, add the pork pieces and cook for 6–8 minutes until well browned and cooked through; do not overcook. Remove from the saucepan and keep warm.

* Heat the remaining oil in the pan, add the ginger and garlic and cook for a couple of minutes. Add the chilli, cumin, coriander and turmeric and lightly fry.

* Add the onion and peppers and stir-fry until slightly wilted. Add the tomato mixture and pork and stir to coat – you may need to add a touch of water. The sauce should coat the vegetable and meat well, like a dry stir-fry. Season with a little sugar and salt and pepper, and add the fresh coriander.

* Serve with boiled or steamed rice and naan bread.

My pork tikka massala

PURISTS WILL POUR SCORN ON THIS RECIPE, BUT IT HAS A GREAT STORY TO IT. REZZA, MY GOOD INDIAN FRIEND AND WONDERFUL CHEF, AND I WERE COOKING IN GLASGOW AT THE SHISH MAHAL, THE RESTAURANT WHERE CHICKEN TIKKA MASSALA WAS INVENTED. ASIF, THE SON OF THE ORIGINAL OWNER, TOLD ME THAT IN THE EARLY 1970S, A BUS DRIVER CAME INTO THE RESTAURANT LATE ONE EVENING. HE ORDERED CHICKEN TIKKA, BUT AFTER A FEW MINUTES SENT IT BACK TO THE KITCHEN SAYING IT WAS DRY. ASIF'S FATHER, RECOVERING FROM AN ULCER AT THE TIME, WAS EATING CANNED SOUP. HE TOLD THE CHEF TO ADD THE CANNED SOUP TO THE TIKKA AND WARM IT THROUGH. THE BUS DRIVER LOVED IT AND THE CHICKEN TIKKA MASALA WAS BORN. TO THIS DAY THE RESTAURANT STILL SERVES THE DISH (BUT NOT WITH CANNED SOUP), AND THEY SELL 25,000 PORTIONS A YEAR. I HAVE RECREATED THE ORIGINAL RECIPE, COMPLETE WITH CANNED SOUP. WHAT FUN!

Serves 4   Preparation time 40 minutes, plus overnight marinating   Cooking time about 45 minutes

2 pork loin fillets, about 350g each, without fat and
    silver sinew, cut into 4cm pieces
salt and freshly ground black pepper

MARINADE
1 tablespoon very finely grated fresh ginger
3 garlic cloves, very finely crushed
2 tablespoons ground coriander
1 tablespoon smoked paprika
2 teaspoons garam masala
1 teaspoon ground cumin
½ teaspoon red chilli powder
2 tablespoons oil (any type will do)
80g thick sheep's milk yogurt

SAUCE
4 tablespoons oil
2 tablespoons ground coriander
4 teaspoons paprika
2 teaspoons ground turmeric
2 teaspoons garam masala
2 teaspoons fenugreek leaves
½ teaspoon ground cloves
4 tablespoons grated fresh ginger
1 small red chilli, very finely chopped
2 large onions, very finely chopped
4 garlic cloves, finely chopped
4 ripe tomatoes, chopped
400g can tomato soup
10g chicken stock cube, crumbled
125ml whipping cream
caster sugar, to taste
50–75g cold unsalted butter, cut into cubes
a few fresh coriander leaves

✱ Put all the marinade ingredients into a glass or ceramic bowl and really mix well. Add the pork pieces and mix well again, adding a little salt and pepper. Cover and leave to marinate in the fridge overnight.

✱ For the sauce, heat the oil in a large pan, add the ground coriander, paprika, turmeric, garam masala, fenugreek, cloves, ginger and chilli and fry for a minute or two. Add the onions and garlic and cook again for a few minutes.

✱ Next, add the tomatoes, soup, stock cube, cream and a little water and cook for 15–20 minutes, or until the onions are cooked and the sauce is slightly reduced.

✱ Meanwhile, preheat a grill to its hottest setting. Blend the sauce in a blender until really smooth, then pour back into the saucepan and bring to a simmer.

✱ Remove the pork from the fridge, place the chunks on a baking tray and grill for 3–4 minutes on each side until half cooked. Place straight into the simmering sauce and simmer for 4–5 minutes to finish cooking; do not overcook. Season well with salt and pepper, and add sugar to balance.

✱ Finally, add the butter and shake the pan until the sauce is thickened and glossy. Add the fresh coriander and serve.

Pork & prawn spring rolls with dipping sauce

SPRING ROLLS ARE EATEN EVERYWHERE IN THE MEKONG DELTA IN SOUTHERN VIETNAM, FILLED WITH MANY VARIETIES OF FISH, HERBS AND VEGETABLES. DURING MY RECENT VISIT TO THE COUNTRY, I ENJOYED A SUPERB EXAMPLE OF THEM IN A TINY RESTAURANT THAT PREPARED THE FISH TO ORDER, FRESH AS A DAISY. SO WITH THAT IN MIND, HERE IS MY VERSION FOR A SNACK OR MAIN COURSE DISH THAT IS DELICIOUS AND VERY EASY TO MAKE AND SERVE, ALONG WITH A LITTLE SWEET AND SOUR DIPPING SAUCE.

Serves 4   Preparation time 20 minutes   Cooking time 15-20 minutes

FILLING

4 large raw freshwater prawns, peeled
1 small pork fillet, about 300-350g,
    without fat or silver sinew
1 teaspoon very finely chopped fresh red chilli
2 teaspoons Vietnamese fish sauce (nuoc cham)
2 heaped teaspoons shrimp paste (optional)
2 garlic cloves, crushed
salt and freshly ground black pepper

DIPPING SAUCE

4 tablespoons soy sauce
1 tablespoon Vietnamese fish sauce (nuoc cham)
1 small red chilli, finely chopped
2 tablespoons chopped fresh coriander
1 tablespoon palm sugar or caster sugar
1 carrot, peeled
4 spring onions
½ small cucumber
16 rice paper pancakes (spring roll wrappers)
1 small bunch fresh Thai basil or any other basil
a few fresh mint leaves
1 small bunch fresh coriander
vegetable oil, for deep-frying

✱ For the filling, chop the prawns and also the pork fillet, the finer the better - if you have a mincer you can use here, then great.

✱ Put the prawn and pork in a bowl, add the chilli, fish sauce, shrimp paste, if using, garlic and salt and pepper, and really mix well.

✱ Next, finely slice the vegetables into thin strips, the thinner the better - matchstick size is about right.

✱ Put all the ingredients for the dipping sauce in a small bowl and mix well.

✱ Lightly wet one side of a rice pancake with a pastry brush or your fingers. Place a small sausage of the prawn and pork mixture on the rice paper, to one side. Top with a few carrot, spring onion and cucumber matchsticks, then add a few leaves of each herb.

✱ Fold the sides of the pancake into the centre and then roll up, making sure that the top lip is wetted again, and seal well. Repeat the process with the remaining rice pancakes.

✱ Heat 2-3cm of vegetable oil in a wok or deep frying pan to about 175°C. Fry the spring rolls in batches of no more than four for about 3-4 minutes, turning once, until crispy and cooked through.

✱ Serve the spring rolls hot with the dipping sauce.

CHAPTER 3 Ham & gammon

Ham, like bacon, is a cured product that is eaten extensively all over the globe, from the world-famous dry-cured hams such as Parma and jamòn Ibérico to the renowned cooked hams like York ham and Wiltshire ham. The word ham generally refers to a cured leg of pork that is ready to eat, whether it is cooked or dry cured. Gammon is a cured leg that will need cooking.

My particular enthusiasm is for producing dry-cured hams that need no cooking after the production process has finished. Many people in the UK have tried to reproduce the flavour of Parma and Ibérico, and failed miserably. With this in mind, I set about trying to produce a British dry-cured ham using continental methods as guidelines, and I have to say that after ten years of tortuous experimentation I have a product that would stand up against any of our European counterparts and that won a major accolade in the UK's leading food award scheme in 2009, the Great Taste Awards.

Cooked hams also remain popular in the modern delicatessen and butcher's shop, though I have to say that the products generally available could only be loosely described as ham. I have seen ham commercially produced where brine is injected into legs of pork at levels of up to 45 per cent and, with the use of functional ingredients such as phosphates, soya protein and carrageenan, will produce cooking yields of up to 120 per cent, which means the finished ham will be 20 per cent heavier than the leg you started with! This, unfortunately, is what happens when supermarkets rule the world with the overwhelming desire to sell the cheapest food. – Simon

Selecting the meat

WHETHER PRODUCING EITHER DRY-CURED OR COOKED HAM, MY MEAT SELECTION PROCESS IS THE SAME:

✱ I use legs from female pigs only that weigh 80–100kg dead weight. Male pigs in the UK are not castrated as a rule and the meat from such animals contains the sex hormones androstenone, testosterone and skatole, which can give an unpleasant flavour to the meat.

✱ The legs should exhibit pH values of 5.5–5.8 or be three days post-slaughter.

✱ I always break the leg down into its different muscles for curing. This helps reduce curing times, and I also prefer the texture of single-muscle products.

CHOOSING A LEG ALSO ENABLES YOU TO PRODUCE MORE THAN ONE KIND OF HAM, AS THE LEG CONSISTS OF FOUR MAJOR MUSCLES:

1 Topside I use this muscle for a cooked ham, as it is lean and tender once cured and cooked.

2 Silverside This is the one I use for a dry-cured ham. It's probably the toughest muscle in the leg, but the dry-curing process and lengthy maturation time, along with enzymatic activity, results in a product that melts in the mouth once cured.

3 Slipper/thick flank This muscle makes a wonderful little cooked ham, especially when flavoured with asparagus.

4 Chump My favourite part of the leg, this makes the most delightful dry-cured ham, especially when lightly smoked over beechwood.

✱ The trimmings can be used for sausages.

DRY*-CURED HAMS
*(AIR)

COPPA ⟫⟫⟫ →

LOMO ⟫⟫⟫ →

Brickhill ham

USE EITHER SILVERSIDE OR CHUMP FOR THIS METHOD. DUE TO THE NATURE OF OUR CLIMATE, YOU MAY SEE MOULD GROWING ON YOUR HAM. THIS WILL NOT AFFECT THE QUALITY OF YOUR HAM AND YOU CAN REMOVE IT BY WIPING THE OUTSIDE OF THE HAM WITH A CLOTH SOAKED IN VINEGAR (WHITE DISTILLED VINEGAR IS FINE).

YOU WILL NEED PER 1KG PORK:

42g curing salt (containing 1% sodium nitrite and 0.8% potassium nitrate)
3g dextrose (the heaviest of the sugars, which helps counteract the toughening effect of the salt)
2g sodium ascorbate (the sodium salt of ascorbic acid, which helps to stabilise the cure colour)
spices/herbs (optional) – black peppercorns, coriander seeds or ground garlic can be added,
   but if you have a nice enough piece of meat to start with, there is no need to flavour it
fibrous casing (man-made casing derived from collagen)
   or ox bung (part of the bovine large intestine), for wrapping the ham

* Mix all the curing ingredients together thoroughly and apply half the mixture to the meat, paying special attention to the thicker parts.

* Place in a suitably sized, robust plastic food container and leave to cure for 7 days in a cold fridge at a temperature of 1–3°C, making sure the meat is turned over at least once. During this time a brine will form in the bottom of the container, which should be discarded at regular intervals.

* After 7 days, apply the rest of the cure mix as before and leave to cure for a further 2 weeks, ensuring that you turn the meat every 2 days.

* After the 2 weeks, wash the ham off in lukewarm water and leave to dry in a cool, airy place for a couple of hours.

* Once dry, the ham can be wrapped in the casing/bung and left to 'equalise' or 'burn through' for a further week in the fridge – this process allows the salt and other additives to diffuse through to the centre of the ham.

* The last step is to hang the ham somewhere cool with little air flow – a cellar or pantry would be ideal – to mature and dry. The ham should be ready to eat when it is quite firm to the touch but not rock hard, 8–12 weeks.

Coppa

This is an Italian speciality made from the neck of the pig rather than silverside or chump.
I actually prefer this to dry-cured ham because it contains a bit more fat and is somewhat sweeter in taste.
It was with this product that I won a three-star gold award at the Great Taste Awards in 2009.
The curing ingredients and method are the same as for dry-cured ham, but you will find that it will
be ready a little sooner than the ham – probably in 6–8 weeks.

Lomo

This Spanish delicacy is made from the eye of the loin. Again, the recipe is the same as for dry-cured ham,
but adding 5g smoked paprika to the cure mix will give it authenticity.

SMOKED HAMS

Kassler

THIS IS A GERMAN SPECIALITY THAT, SADLY, IS NOT AS POPULAR IN THE UK AS IT SHOULD BE. WHEN MADE CORRECTLY IT IS ABSOLUTELY DELICIOUS, WHETHER HOT OR COLD.

YOU WILL NEED PER 1KG BONELESS, RINDLESS LOIN:

500ml water
50g curing salt (containing 0.6% sodium nitrite and 0.8% potassium nitrate)
2g dextrose
1g sodium ascorbate

✱ Mix the brine ingredients together thoroughly in a large, deep, strong plastic or stainless steel bowl or container – the easiest way is to use warm water and then chill the brine, but you can use cold water if you prefer.

✱ Immerse the loin in the brine so that it is completely covered. Leave in the fridge for a week.

✱ Remove the ham from the brine and leave in a cool, airy place for a further 2 days until it is dry to the touch.

✱ Apply a light smoke (see page 107), setting the smoker for indirect cooking at a temperature of 78°C and cooking until a core of 68°C is reached.

Westphalian-style ham

A TRUE WESTPHALIAN HAM IS A TOP-QUALITY AIR-DRIED SMOKED HAM FROM GERMANY. IN MY VERSION, I USE THE SAME CURING METHOD AS FOR THE BRICKHILL HAM (SEE PAGE 81). I USUALLY SMOKE THE HAM FOR ABOUT 30 MINUTES AND THEN, INSTEAD OF THE LENGTHY DRYING PERIOD, STEAM COOK AT A TEMPERATURE OF 78°C UNTIL A CORE TEMPERATURE OF 68°C IS REACHED.

COOKED HAMS

Brine curing

USE TOPSIDE, THICK FLANK OR HAM HOCKS. YOU WILL NEED A QUANTITY OF BRINE
APPROXIMATELY HALF THE WEIGHT OF THE HAM, AS FOLLOWS:

YOU WILL NEED PER 1KG PORK:

300ml water
80g curing salt (containing 0.6% sodium nitrite and 0.8% potassium nitrate)
20g sodium ascorbate
100g ice

✱ Mix the brine ingredients together thoroughly in a large,
deep strong plastic or stainless steel bowl or container – the
easiest way is to use warm water and mix in the curing salt
and sodium ascorbate, then add the ice.

✱ Take your selected muscle and ensure that it is trimmed of
all visible gristle and sinew. Immerse the ham in the brine so
that it is completely covered. Leave in the fridge for a week.

✱ Remove the ham from the brine and leave to dry off in
a cool, airy place for a further 2 days before cooking. Phil's
recipe for Baked Brown Sugar Glazed Ham Hocks with
Cloves, Tamarind and English Mustard (see page 86) is my
particular favourite.

Asparagus ham

You will need the same ingredients for the brine as above
but with the addition of 4–5g asparagus flavouring
(a totally natural brine additive available from good butchers)
per 1kg meat.

Burgundy ham

Again, the recipe is the same as above but with the addition
of 4–5g burgundy flavouring (a totally natural brine additive
available from good butchers) to the brine per 1kg meat.

Baked brown sugar glazed ham hocks with cloves, tamarind & English mustard

I COOKED THIS ON TELLY SOME YEARS AGO AND IT'S BEEN A CHRISTMAS FAVOURITE EVER SINCE. THE SKIN AND FAT TAKE ON A REALLY POWERFUL FLAVOUR, AND THEY LOOK STUNNING.

Serves 6–8   Preparation time 20 minutes, plus overnight soaking, then chilling   Cooking time about 3 hours in total

4 brined ham hocks (see page 85)
2 carrots, peeled but left whole
2 celery sticks
½ leek, washed well but left whole
2 onions, peeled but left whole
2 tablespoons black peppercorns
4 bay leaves
1 head of garlic
salt (optional)

GLAZE
400g dark muscovado sugar
350ml dry cider
4 tablespoons tamarind paste
4 tablespoons olive oil
100g runny honey
2 tablespoons English mustard/ English mustard powder
1 tablespoon smoked paprika
1 teaspoon ground cloves

✱ Soak the hocks in cold water overnight.

✱ Drain the hocks and wash them really well, then place in a deep pan. Fill with cold water and bring to the boil. Reduce the heat and simmer for 5 minutes, then taste the water: if it's salty, tip away the water and refill, but if okay, add a little salt to the water.

✱ Reduce the heat still further until the water is just simmering and cook for 15 minutes. Skim off any scum, then add all the veg, peppercorns and herbs. Cook for a further 2 hours 15 minutes.

✱ Turn the heat off and leave the hocks to cool, then chill in the fridge in their stock.

✱ The next day, preheat the oven to 200°C/Gas 6.

✱ Lift the chilled hocks out of the jellied stock and rinse off any jelly clinging to the hocks.

✱ Leaving the large bone in the joint, pull out the second smaller bone, then trim off the rind and discard. Lightly score the meat that's left and place on a non-stick baking tray.

✱ Mix all the glaze ingredients together really well, then pour over the hocks and place in the hot oven. Cook for 20–25 minutes, spooning the glaze over repeatedly until well glazed.

✱ Serve in deep bowls and just pull off the meat in large chunks. I eat this hot or cold with buttery mashed potatoes.

Baked gammon with spicy squash chutney »»→

Baked gammon with spicy squash chutney

THIS IS AN UNUSUAL WAY OF COOKING HAM. IT DOES TAKE A BIT OF TIME BUT IS WELL WORTH THE EFFORT – GREAT EATEN HOT OR COLD FOR BREAKFAST OR BRUNCH.

Serves 4–6   Preparation time 30 minutes   Cooking time about 2 hours 45 minutes–3 hours 15 minutes

about 750g plain flour
250g salt
about 10 large egg whites
1.5kg smoked gammon joint, rind on, soaked overnight and
    dried well
4 tablespoons runny honey
1 tablespoon molasses
1 teaspoon ground allspice

CHUTNEY
4 tablespoons good-quality olive oil
1 teaspoon caraway seeds
1 teaspoon crushed juniper berries
1 teaspoon whole cloves
2 small red onions, finely chopped
2 garlic cloves, crushed
1 tablespoon finely chopped fresh ginger
450g peeled and deseeded squash
140ml cider vinegar
2 tablespoons Worcestershire sauce
175g soft light brown sugar
salt and freshly ground black pepper

* Soak the hocks in cold water overnight. Drain and dry well.

* Preheat the oven to 160°C/Gas 3.

* Sift the flour and salt into a bowl and stir in enough egg white to form a stiff dough. I keep leftover egg whites in the freezer, and this is a good way of using them up.

* Sit the ham on a thick wedge of scrunched-up foil in a roasting tray. Roll out the dough carefully on a lightly floured surface to a rectangle large enough to cover the top and sides of the joint. Lay the dough over the gammon, then tuck under the joint and press the edges together to seal well, ensuring the whole gammon is encased. Make a small incision in the top to let out the steam.

* Bake for about 2 hours 30 minutes–3 hours. To check if it is cooked, insert a skewer through the vent – there should be little resistance but the meat shouldn't be too firm.

* Meanwhile, for the chutney, heat the olive oil in a large pan. Add the caraway seeds, juniper berries, cloves, onions, garlic and ginger and cook for about 6–8 minutes – you'll get a wonderful smell all around the kitchen.

* Add the squash, vinegar, Worcestershire sauce and sugar, stir in and season well. Then cook slowly for about 15–20 minutes until the squash is tender and the consistency of the chutney is nice and thick. Leave to cool.

* Mix the honey, molasses and allspice together and set aside.

* When the ham is cooked, remove the crust and discard. Years ago, some of the crust would have been grated and placed on top of the cooked joint (the forerunner to breadcrumbs). Cut away all the rind and a little fat from the gammon.

* Place the gammon in a clean non-stick roasting tray, cut the fat into a crisscross pattern and pour over the honey and molasses mixture.

* Increase the oven temperature to 220°C/Gas 7 and slide the ham back into the oven to glaze nicely. Bake for about 15–20 minutes – take care, otherwise it will catch and burn.

* Cut the gammon into thick slices and serve with the chutney or the compote on page 93.

Griddled gammon steak with spicy chickpea & tomato stew

I REALLY LIKE GAMMON STEAKS. YES, I LIKE THEM WITH PINEAPPLE AND I ALSO LIKE THEM WITH FRIED EGGS AND CHIPS. MY DAUGHTER ADORES THEM, BUT THE GAMMON HAS TO BE OF GOOD QUALITY, OTHERWISE THEY ARE TOO SALTY AND HAVE NO FLAVOUR. I ESPECIALLY LIKE THE RIM OF FAT; IT'S DELICIOUS AND WHEN DRY-CURED THE RIND WILL BUBBLE UP BEAUTIFULLY. HERE I HAVE ADDED A CHICKPEA AND TOMATO STEW, BOTH EASY AND FILLING.

Serves 4   Preparation time 10 minutes   Cooking time 15 minutes

4 gammon steaks, about 275g each

STEW
4 tablespoons olive oil
2 onions, finely chopped
2 garlic cloves, chopped
400g can chopped tomatoes in juice
400g can chickpeas, drained
pinch of dried chilli flakes
½ x 10g chicken or vegetable stock cube
200ml cold water
2 tablespoons vinegar (any type)
1 tablespoon caster sugar
4 gammon steaks, about 275g each
salt and freshly ground black pepper

* Heat the oil in a saucepan, add the onions and garlic and soften for a couple of minutes.

* Add all the remaining ingredients except the gammon and simmer for 10–15 minutes or so until the mixture thickens. Season well and add a little more olive oil if needed; the sauce should be glossy.

* Meanwhile, griddle or grill the steaks for 4–5 minutes on each side until cooked through, but don't overcook.

* To serve, pile the chickpea stew into the middle of four bowls and top each with a gammon steak.

* This stew is also great cold with crusty bread as a dip or as a topping.

Baked gammon with tomato compote

THE VICTORIANS LIKED SAVOURY COMPOTES, ESPECIALLY AT BREAKFAST TIME, AND HERE IS A TOMATO ONE THAT I HAVE COOKED FOR YEARS, TO SERVE AS AN ALTERNATIVE ACCOMPANIMENT TO THE BAKED GAMMON ON PAGE 90.

Serves 4-6   Preparation time 30 minutes   Cooking time about 2 hours 45 minutes–3 hours 15 minutes

1 quantity Baked Gammon (see page 90)

COMPOTE
100ml cold water
100ml cider vinegar
75g unrefined granulated sugar
1 teaspoon caraway seeds
1 cinnamon stick
2 shallots, finely chopped
500g cherry tomatoes
2 tablespoons chopped tarragon

✱ While the gammon is baking, prepare the compote. Put the water, vinegar, sugar, caraway seeds, cinnamon stick and shallots into a saucepan and bring to the boil, then reduce the heat and simmer for 2 minutes. Add the tomatoes and cook for 1 minute, or until the skins just start to split. Turn off the heat and cover with clingfilm. Leave to cool. When cool, add the chopped tarragon.

✱ Cut the baked and glazed gammon into thick slices and serve with the compote, and perhaps a fried egg or two.

Ham hock salad with English mustard & lentil dressing

THIS DRESSING MUST BE MADE THE DAY BEFORE YOU NEED IT; IF YOU MAKE IT AND EAT IT STRAIGHT AWAY, IT'S AWFUL, BUT IF YOU LEAVE THE DRESSING FOR 24 HOURS, THE FLAVOUR CHANGES DRAMATICALLY, BELIEVE ME. MUSTARD POWDER LOSES ITS PUNGENCY SOON AFTER YOU ADD LIQUID, SO IT'S BEST TO LEAVE THIS IN OVERNIGHT, BUT RE-SEASON WITH SALT AND PEPPER, SUGAR AND VINEGAR THE NEXT DAY. WARM THE SMALL CHUNKS OF SUCCULENT HAM HOCK IN THE DRESSING.

Serves 4   Preparation time 20 minutes, plus cooling/chilling   Cooking time 2 hours 40 minutes

2 brined ham hocks (see page 85)
1 teaspoon black peppercorns
3 bay leaves
salt and freshly ground black pepper

DRESSING
2 egg yolks
2 heaped tablespoons English mustard powder
caster sugar, to taste
3 tablespoons white wine vinegar
300ml vegetable oil
25ml cold water
4 shallots, finely sliced (not chopped)

4 heaped tablespoons fresh mixed herbs, such as basil, flat-leaf parsley, chives, chervil and tarragon
150g cooked green lentils

TO SERVE
1 small bag watercress
1 small Cos (Romaine) or Iceberg lettuce, chopped
4 tomatoes, cut into chunks
boiled new potatoes (if serving as a main course)

✱ Soak the ham hocks in cold water for 24 hours, changing the water occasionally.

✱ Drain the hocks and put into a large saucepan with plenty of fresh cold water. Bring to the boil and then you really must reduce to a simmer, not keep at a raging boil, or the meat will become tough and stringy, especially the outside 3–4cm. A good tip here is to taste the water after simmering for 5 minutes. If it's salty, tip out the water and start again; if not, add a little salt and the peppercorns and bay leaves. Then simmer the hocks for 2 hours 30 minutes exactly.

✱ Remove the pan from the hob and leave the hocks to cool in the liquor, then chill in the fridge in the stock until cold.

✱ To prepare the hocks, remove them from the jelly and wash off under warm water. Remove all the skin and gristle, and pull the lobes of meat off the bone. Remove most of the fat and cut the meat into bite-sized pieces.

✱ For the dressing, put the egg yolks, mustard powder, salt and pepper, sugar and vinegar in a bowl. Whisk together, then gradually add the vegetable oil until completely emulsified. Check the seasoning and adjust if necessary. Also add the cold water to form a thick, but not too thick, mayonnaise. Stir in the shallots, herbs and lentils.

✱ Cover and place the dressing in the fridge, leaving it overnight if possible. Then check the seasoning and adjust, with sugar, vinegar, salt and pepper, stirring well.

✱ To serve, pour some of the dressing into a small pan, add a few pieces of ham hock and warm through gently. Spoon over a mixture of watercress and lettuce and mix well but carefully, pile onto a plate and serve warm with the tomatoes. For a main, serve with boiled new potatoes.

Easy potato & ham hash with rocket & apple salad

I LOVE HASH IN ANY FORM – NORMALLY BEEF IS USED, AND CORNED BEEF AT THAT. HERE IS A HAM VERSION THAT IS BOTH DELICIOUS AND REALLY EASY TO MAKE. I USE LEFTOVER ROAST POTATOES, BUT ANY COOKED POTATO WILL DO.

Serves 4   Preparation time 20 minutes   Cooking time about 30 minutes

4 tablespoons olive oil
1 onion, cut into 2cm chunks
2 large carrots, peeled, cooked and cut into small pieces
8 leftover or cooked roast potatoes, cut into small chunks
½ cauliflower, broken into florets, then cooked
10g chicken stock cube, crumbled
100ml water
200g cooked ham, cut into cooked 1cm cubes
freshly ground black pepper
4 fried eggs, to serve

SALAD
140g rocket (2 bags)
2 small eating apples, such as Cox's
1 small red onion, finely sliced
2 tablespoons olive oil
squeeze of lemon juice

✱ Heat the olive oil in a large, non-stick frying pan with a tight-fitting lid. Add the onion and cook for a few minutes to brown slightly.

✱ Add the carrots, potatoes and cauliflower to the pan, and continue to cook until they all take on a little colour.

✱ Next, add the crumbled stock cube, water, cubed ham and a generous dash of pepper, then bring to the boil. Stir well, cover with the lid and cook over a low heat for 20 minutes.

✱ When the vegetables are cooked, check the seasoning and adjust if necessary, then keep warm.

✱ For the salad, place the rocket in a large bowl, then grate the apples on a coarse grater, with the skin on. Add to the rocket and onion and mix well but lightly.

✱ Add the olive oil and lemon juice, and mix well again, but be careful not to crush the rocket.

✱ Serve the hash in deep bowls, each topped with a fried egg, with the salad separately.

Pork osso bucco

I COOKED THIS RECIPE MANY YEARS AGO IN THE PUB. I WAS LOOKING FOR SOMETHING THAT USED A CHEAPER CUT OF MEAT AND THIS DISH CAME TO MIND. THE GOOD THING IS THAT IT CAN BE SIMMERED ON TOP OF THE STOVE VERY GENTLY, SO THE OVEN CAN STAY OFF, SAVING POWER. DO SIMMER IT VERY GENTLY; IT WILL MAKE ALL THE DIFFERENCE. I USE SOME OF THE BRAISING LIQUOR IN THE FINAL SAUCE, SO BEWARE OF SEASONING TOO HIGHLY AT THE START.

Serves 4   Preparation time 30 minutes, cooling/chilling
Cooking time 2 hours 40 minutes for the osso buccos, 1 hour–1 hour 10 minutes to finish

8 pork osso bucco joints (5cm-thick slices of uncured
    pork hock – I reckon 1 hock per serving)
about 600ml strong chicken stock (you may need less)
1 onion, finely chopped
1 carrot, peeled and finely chopped
1 celery stick, finely chopped
1 small sprig of fresh thyme
2 sprigs of fresh sage
2 garlic cloves, crushed
a few black peppercorns
pinch of salt

SAUCE
4 tablespoons olive oil
2 onions, finely chopped
4 garlic cloves, chopped or crushed
400g can chopped tomatoes in juice
185g jar roasted peppers, drained and cut into
    2cm cubes or slices
2 tablespoons tomato purée
2 x 10g chicken stock cubes
250ml pork stock from cooking the osso bucco
150ml dry white wine
50ml sherry vinegar
25g caster sugar
100ml whipping cream
30g watercress, roughly chopped
salt and freshly ground black pepper

✳ Remove the rind and a little of the fat from the hock slices.

✳ Put the hock slices in a deep saucepan so that they fit nice and snugly. Cover with the stock until they are submerged by say 2–3cm, and then add the vegetables, herbs, garlic, peppercorns and salt.

✳ Bring to the boil and skim well, then cover, reduce the heat right down and just simmer, very slowly, for 2 hours 30 minutes, or until the meat is tender, succulent, but not falling off the bone.

✳ Once cooked, cool and chill well in the stock. When ready to finish the dish, remove the hock slices from the stock and measure out 250ml of the stock for the sauce.

✳ To make the sauce, heat the olive oil in a saucepan, add the onions and garlic and cook for 5 minutes to soften.

✳ Add all the remaining ingredients except the cream and watercress. Season, then simmer gently for about 35–40 minutes until reduced and a nice sauce consistency.

✳ Add the cream and cook for a further 5 minutes. Finally, add the watercress and mix well, then re-season and taste to check the seasoning.

✳ Put the cooked osso buccos in a shallow saucepan and cover with the sauce, then simmer with the lid on for 15–20 minutes to warm through. Alternatively, put into an ovenproof dish, cover and pop in the oven preheated to 180°C/Gas 4 to heat through.

✳ Serve with steamed green vegetables such as beans, cabbage or the best of spring greens.

CHAPTER 4 Bacon & pancetta

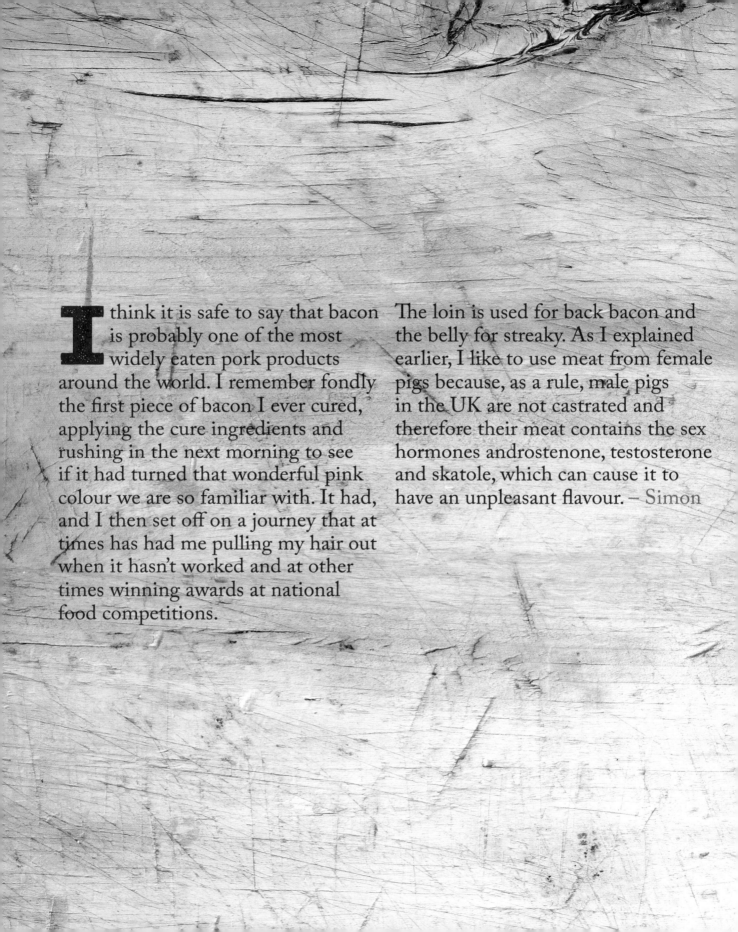

I think it is safe to say that bacon is probably one of the most widely eaten pork products around the world. I remember fondly the first piece of bacon I ever cured, applying the cure ingredients and rushing in the next morning to see if it had turned that wonderful pink colour we are so familiar with. It had, and I then set off on a journey that at times has had me pulling my hair out when it hasn't worked and at other times winning awards at national food competitions.

The loin is used for back bacon and the belly for streaky. As I explained earlier, I like to use meat from female pigs because, as a rule, male pigs in the UK are not castrated and therefore their meat contains the sex hormones androstenone, testosterone and skatole, which can cause it to have an unpleasant flavour. – Simon

WHETHER MAKING BACK OR STREAKY BACON, THE THREE MAIN PROCESSES REMAIN THE SAME:

Dry curing

The meat is rubbed with a mixture of curing salt, sugar and sometimes spices. This mixture diffuses through the meat over a period of time, thereby curing the meat. This method is the slowest, but it produces the best-quality bacon.

Brine curing

Instead of the curing ingredients being applied directly to the meat, they are mixed with water to make a brine. The meat is then added and left to cure through. Again, this is a reasonably slow method that produces a quality product.

Brine injection

This method employs the use of a needle injector to force the brine into the meat. It's by far the fastest way to produce bacon and is the method most commonly used by the big bacon producers, as it results in a cheap product in a short space of time – as little as 48 hours. In my opinion, the word 'quality' should not be used to describe the end product.

DRY CURING

This is my chosen method of curing bacon. Use loins or bellies ideally weighing 80–100kg. I prefer to use pigs of this size because they will give a fuller loin and belly so that after curing you are left with bacon rashers that are of a decent size. If using a pH meter when selecting your meat, which I highly recommend, it needs to register between 5.5 and 5.8. This pH is usually reached three days after slaughter and is also an indication that microbiological growth is controlled. – Simon

Back bacon

YOU WILL NEED PER 1KG PORK LOIN:

42g curing salt (containing 1% sodium nitrite and 0.8% potassium nitrate)
3g dextrose (the heaviest of the sugars, which helps counteract the toughening effect of the salt)
2g sodium ascorbate (the sodium salt of ascorbic acid, which helps to stabilise the cure colour)
0.5–1g spice – black peppercorns, coriander seeds, juniper berries and bay leaves all lend themselves to dry-cure mixes

✱ Mix these ingredients together thoroughly and apply to the pork, making sure the thickest part of meat receives the most amount of salt. Ensure that the whole piece of meat is covered with the mixture.

✱ Place in a suitably sized, robust plastic food container and leave to cure for 10 days in a cold fridge at a temperature of 1–3°C. During this time a brine will form in the bottom of the container, which should be discarded at regular intervals.

✱ After the 10 days, wash the bacon off in lukewarm water and leave to dry for a couple of hours in a cool, airy place.

✱ At this point you can smoke the bacon if you wish. If you do, the bacon needs to reach ambient temperature beforehand or you will get condensation and it will not smoke properly.

✱ Depending on the kind of smoker you have, the cooler the smoke, the better your bacon will be; I would recommend a smoking temperature of no higher than 42°C. Alternatively, simply leave it as it is.

✱ To keep your bacon in pristine condition, either vacuum pack it – a friendly butcher would do this for you I'm sure – or wrap the whole piece in greaseproof paper and keep in the fridge. Your bacon will improve with age, as the dehydration process intensifies its flavour, especially if you have used spices in your cure mix. You can then slice it as thickly or thinly as you prefer.

✱ Finally, and most importantly, when you get to make your first butty with your homemade bacon, please refrain from putting ketchup on it! I can cope with a small amount of brown sauce, but definitely not ketchup.

Streaky bacon

THE ONLY CHANGE TO THE INGREDIENTS ABOVE FOR CURING BELLY TO MAKE STREAKY BACON IS THE AMOUNT OF SALT REQUIRED – USE 32G CURING SALT PER 1KG BONELESS PORK BELLY. THE CURING TIME CAN BE SHORTENED TO 7 DAYS, BUT OTHERWISE FOLLOW THE METHOD FOR BACK BACON ABOVE.

HOME SMOKING

The smell of fresh smoked bacon is every bit as appealing as the smell of freshly made bread. Although the practice of smoking food has been going on for more than 80,000 years, it's not as easy as one might think, and indeed is something of an art form. I use a commercially made smokehouse with hardwood chips such as beech and oak to smoke all of my products. It has a microprocessor to control every step of the smoking process, which ensures that my products are consistent every time. Home smoking, however, is a different kettle of fish, being more of a case of trial and error. There are many smokers available to buy for home use, and many people devise their own smoking kit using old refrigerators and dustbins. But as long as you are willing to persevere and record your methods, there is no reason why you shouldn't be successful.

To smoke your own bacon, you need to make sure that the bacon is sufficiently dry to take the smoke – it's advisable to allow your product to reach the same temperature as your smoker to avoid condensation. Depending on the smoker you are using, you can choose how long to smoke your bacon to achieve the desired colour and flavour. – Simon

Smoked pancetta

THIS ITALIAN DELICACY, WHEN MADE PROPERLY, IS VERY DIFFERENT FROM WHAT IS GENERALLY OFFERED FOR SALE IN THE UK. SMOKED STREAKY BACON IS OFTEN SOLD AS PANCETTA AND, ALTHOUGH IT'S DELICIOUS, IT ISN'T PANCETTA. PANCETTA IS A CURED PORK BELLY MARINATED WITH HERBS AND SPICES, ROLLED AND TIED AND THEN STUFFED INTO A PERMEABLE CASING AND HUNG UP TO MATURE AND DRY MUCH LIKE A COPPA OR LOMO (SEE PAGE 81).

Makes 1kg

40g curing salt (containing 1% sodium nitrite and 0.8% potassium nitrate)
3g dextrose
2g sodium ascorbate
6g dried thyme
4g ground black pepper
4g ground garlic
1 kg boneless, rindless pork belly or pig cheek (jowl)
fibrous casing (man-made casing derived from collagen), optional

✱ Mix all the dry ingredients together thoroughly and rub into both sides of the pork belly.

✱ Roll the belly into a cylindrical shape and tie to hold the shape. Leave to cure for a week in the fridge and then stuff into casing or wrap up in a pave. Tie really tightly and prick with a needle to get rid of any air pockets.

✱ Apply a light smoke and hang up to dry in an environment with a temperature of 12–14°C and a relative humidity of 75–78 per cent. It will be ready when quite firm to the touch, which will be in about 8–12 weeks' time.

Chilli bacon

THIS BACON GIVES A LOVELY SPICY TWIST TO THE CLASSIC BLT (SEE PAGE 117). FOLLOW THE RECIPE FOR STREAKY BACON ON PAGE 105 BUT ADD 5G SMOKED PAPRIKA AND 2G CHILLI POWDER TO THE CURE BLEND.

Brickhill black bacon

THIS IS ONE OF THE SPECIALITIES OF THE HOUSE – SIMPLY DELICIOUS.

YOU WILL NEED PER 1KG DRY-CURED BACON:

400ml water

100g molasses sugar or black treacle

50g curing salt (containing 0.6% sodium nitrite and 0.8% potassium nitrate)

✱ Mix the brine ingredients together thoroughly in a large, deep, strong plastic or stainless steel bowl or container – the easiest way is to use warm water and then chill the brine.

✱ Immerse your dry-cured bacon in the brine for 2–3 days, keeping it in the fridge – it should go nice and dark during this time.

✱ Remove the bacon and leave to dry for a couple of hours in a cool, airy place.

✱ Give the bacon a good smoke, after which it will resemble a large lump of coal. However, it will make the finest bacon sandwiches you have ever eaten.

American-style streaky bacon

THE BEAUTY OF THIS TYPE OF BACON IS THAT WHEN YOU GRILL OR FRY IT, IT STAYS FLAT AND GOES REALLY CRISPY, JUST AS YOU WOULD FIND IN A NEW YORK DINER.

YOU WILL NEED PER 1KG BONELESS PORK BELLY:

500ml water

60g curing salt (containing 0.6% sodium nitrite and 0.8% potassium nitrate)

4g dextrose

4g sodium ascorbate

✱ Mix the brine ingredients together thoroughly in a large, deep, strong plastic or stainless steel bowl or container – the easiest way is to use warm water and then chill the brine.

✱ Immerse the belly in the brine for about 3–4 days, keeping it in the fridge.

✱ Remove the bacon and leave to dry for a couple of hours in a cool, airy place.

✱ Place the bacon in a smoker and hot smoke at 65°C until the core of the product reaches 55°C. Chill well and then slice thinly.

Smoked pig cheek pancetta with mussels & orzo

THE CHEEK OR JOWL IS A SOMETIMES FORGOTTEN PART OF THE ANIMAL, USUALLY ADDED TO SAUSAGES. HOWEVER, IT MAKES A GREAT PANCETTA WITH JUST THE RIGHT AMOUNT OF FAT. ADDING A LIGHT SMOKE ENHANCES THE FLAVOUR EVEN FURTHER. THE ADDITION OF A RICH TOMATO SAUCE AND A FEW LIGHTLY STEAMED MUSSELS MAKES A PERFECTLY BALANCED, SLIGHTLY DIFFERENT DISH.

Serves 4   Preparation time 20 minutes   Cooking time 30 minutes

4 tablespoons olive oil
350g smoked cheek pancetta (see page 109),
   or use standard pancetta or smoked bacon, very thinly sliced
250g cooked orzo pasta
350g cooked shelled mussels
4 tablespoons chopped fresh basil
4 tablespoons chopped fresh flat-leaf parsley
salt and freshly ground black pepper

SAUCE
4 tablespoons olive oil
1 large onion, finely chopped
2 garlic cloves, chopped
1 glass dry white wine
2 tablespoons tomato purée
400g can chopped tomatoes in juice
2 ripe fresh tomatoes, chopped
2 tablespoons white or red wine vinegar
10g vegetable stock cube, crumbled
1 tablespoon caster sugar

* For the sauce, heat the olive oil in a saucepan, add the onion and garlic and cook for 3–4 minutes.

* Add the wine and tomato purée and cook for a further 5 minutes, then add all the remaining sauce ingredients and season with salt and pepper. Cook down slowly for 10 minutes until thick and pulpy.

* Heat the olive oil in a wok or deep frying pan. Add the pancetta and stir-fry for 2–3 minutes, then stir in the tomato sauce and simmer for 5 minutes.

* Add the cooked orzo and mussels and just warm through. Finally, add the fresh herbs and season well. Serve asap.

Simple spaghetti with pancetta, mozzarella, peas & olive oil

THIS BRILLIANT GREEN, TASTY SAUCE FOR SPAGHETTI IS SIMPLY MADE FROM FROZEN PEAS, VEGETABLE STOCK, FRESH MINT AND EXTRA VIRGIN OLIVE OIL, COMBINED WITH PANCETTA AND TOPPED WITH MOZZARELLA. THE END RESULT IS SURPRISINGLY GOOD, TRUST ME. PANCETTA, LIKE STREAKY BACON, IS SALT-CURED BELLY OF PORK OR CHEEK, BUT IS SOMETIMES FLAVOURED WITH HERBS AND ROLLED, AND AS WITH BACON IT CAN BE LIGHTLY SMOKED.

Serves 4   Preparation time 15 minutes   Cooking time 15 minutes

300g dried spaghetti (this will give you 900g cooked)
200g pancetta, very finely chopped
2 garlic cloves, crushed
250g frozen peas
4 tablespoons extra virgin olive oil
10g vegetable stock cube, dissolved in about 100ml boiling water
4 tablespoons chopped fresh mint
250g pack fresh mozzarella, drained and diced
salt and freshly ground black pepper

✱ Cook the spaghetti in a large saucepan of boiling water until just tender, then drain and keep hot.

✱ Heat a frying pan, add the pancetta and cook until light and crispy. Add the garlic and cook, stirring, for 2 minutes.

✱ Meanwhile, cook the peas in plenty of salted boiling water for 2–3 minutes, then drain and keep warm.

✱ Pop half the peas into a blender, or crush with the back of a fork. Add the olive oil and blitz or mix, gradually adding enough of the stock to give you a nice sauce-like purée.

✱ Add the mint to the cooked spaghetti, along with the remaining whole peas and the cooked pancetta and garlic. Then add the hot pea sauce, stir well and season with salt and pepper. Add the diced mozzarella and mix well.

✱ Serve with a simple tomato salad and garlic bread.

Bacon-aise sandwiches

I FIRST COOKED THIS DISH FOR THE FALKLAND ISLANDS VETERANS AT LIBERTY LODGE IN STANLEY ON A VISIT TO MARK THE 30TH ANNIVERSARY OF THE CONFLICT. IT WAS A COLD, WET AND WINDY DAY AND THIS REALLY HIT THE SPOT. THE ADDED BONUS IS THAT IT USES INGREDIENTS YOU WOULD USUALLY HAVE TO HAND.

Serves 4   Preparation time 10 minutes   Cooking time 15 minutes

16 streaky bacon rashers, 8 fried until really crisp,
    and 8 cooked in the normal way, kept warm
6 tablespoons mayonnaise
1 scant tablespoon mango chutney or marmalade
1 tablespoon roughly chopped fresh flat-leaf parsley
1 heaped teaspoon prepared English mustard
8 slices seeded bread (any type will do)

✱ Finely chop the very crisp bacon and pop into a bowl.

✱ Next, add the mayo, chutney or marmalade, parsley and mustard and really mix well.

✱ Spread the bacon-aise liberally onto the bread slices. Top four of the bread slices with two warm bacon rashers, then top with the remaining bread slices, bacon-aise-side down. Cut in half and serve.

Devils on horseback

I ONCE WORKED IN A HOTEL THAT SERVED SAVOURIES AFTER DESSERT. IT WAS A REAL PAIN BECAUSE YOU FINISHED WORKING A GOOD HOUR AFTER EVERYONE ELSE. HOWEVER, IT WAS NICE TO SERVE CLASSIC DISHES LIKE THE ONE BELOW, WHICH REPUTEDLY FIRST APPEARED IN MRS BEETON'S BOOK OF HOUSEHOLD MANAGEMENT IN 1888. THE PÂTÉ MAKES A BIG DIFFERENCE, GIVING THE END RESULT A MORE ROUNDED FLAVOUR PROFILE.

Serves 4   Preparation time 10 minutes   Cooking time 10 minutes

8 ready-to-eat pitted prunes
100g any pâté (shop-bought Brussels is fine)
8 dry-cured smoked streaky bacon rashers, cut as thinly as possible
2 tablespoons olive oil
1 lemon, halved, for squeezing over

✱ Open out the prunes slightly and spoon a little pâté into each, then close over as best as possible.

✱ Lay the bacon out on a chopping board and place a prune on the bottom of each rasher. Roll up and secure with a half a wooden cocktail stick.

✱ Heat the olive oil in a non-stick frying pan, add the rolls and cook for 2–3 minutes on each side. Serve warm with a squeeze of lemon.

American-style cured bacon BLT

THE COMBINATION OF CRISP BACON, SOFT BREAD, CRUNCHY LETTUCE AND SWEET TOMATO IS A PERFECT MATCH OF TEXTURES AND FLAVOURS, AND THE CONTRAST OF HOT BACON WITH COLD SALAD IS VERY SATISFYING. BUT HERE'S A TWIST ON THE GREAT CLASSIC. HEAT-CURED CRISP BACON (SEE PAGE 110) MAKES ALL THE DIFFERENCE AND, COUPLED WITH THE 'CORONATION' MAYO, MOVES THE BLT ON A STAGE. HEAT-CURED BACON CRISPS UP MORE EVENLY, MAKING THE SANDWICH MUCH NICER TO EAT, AND THE 'CORONATION' MAYO IS A TIME-HONOURED RECIPE THAT USES A SWEETENED CURRY POWDER SUPPOSEDLY INVENTED TO CELEBRATE QUEEN ELIZABETH II'S CORONATION.

Serves 2   Preparation time 15 minutes   Cooking time 15 minutes

8 American-style cured bacon rashers
6 slices granary or malted bread
50g soft butter
4 tablespoons mayonnaise
1 tablespoon runny honey
½ teaspoon Madras curry paste
1 tablespoon chopped chives
2 large ripe plum tomatoes, thickly sliced
75g Cos (Romaine) lettuce, finely shredded
freshly ground black pepper

* Grill or fry the bacon until crisp but not burnt.

* Toast the bread on both sides, then butter well.

* Place two slices of toast on a board and arrange four bacon rashers on each.

* Mix the mayo, honey and curry paste together well, then add the chives. Spoon half the mayo onto the bacon, then top with tomato slices.

* Add another slice of buttered toast to each sandwich, then the shredded lettuce and the remaining half of the mayo mixture. Season with a little pepper and top with the last pieces of toast.

* Cut into quarters on the diagonal, then secure each quarter with a cocktail stick. Serve warm.

Smoked bacon, sweet turnip & potatoes

I COOKED THIS DISH FOR THE FIRST TIME ON A BEACH IN NORTHERN NORWAY LAST YEAR. IT'S A VERY SIMPLE DISH BUT IT WORKS REALLY WELL, ESPECIALLY IF YOU ENSURE THAT THE BEST-QUALITY PORK IS USED. I ALSO ADDED SOME KING CRAB THAT I HAD CAUGHT AND SIMMERED IN SEA WATER RIGHT ON THE WATER'S EDGE, ITS SWEETNESS, AS WITH THAT OF THE TURNIP, GOING PERFECTLY WITH THE SMOKY BACON. SWEET TURNIPS ARE SOMETIMES EATEN RAW IN NORWAY, LIKE AN APPLE, BUT HERE I'VE COOKED THEM.

Serves 4   Preparation time 20 minutes   Cooking time 20–25 minutes

500g slab smoked pork belly or bacon, chopped into 2-3cm pieces
1 large onion, chopped
2 garlic cloves, crushed
500g baby new potatoes, boiled and halved
250g small sweet turnips, boiled, peeled and halved
6 tablespoons mayonnaise
4 tablespoons chopped fresh dill
salt and freshly ground black pepper

✱ Place a large dry sauté pan on the hob and heat until fairly hot.

✱ Add the pork belly or bacon to the hot pan. Cook for 5–6 minutes until the bacon has taken on a little colour and the fat is starting to run. Remove from the pan and keep warm.

✱ Add the onion and garlic to the pan and again cook until a little colour has been taken on, then add the potatoes and turnips and stir well.

✱ Return the meat to the pan and cook for 10 minutes, nice and gently. More fat will run, which is what you want, ensuring that all the ingredients take on a lovely colour and are cooked through. Season well with pepper and a little salt.

✱ Remove the pan from the heat and spoon the contents into a large bowl, then dot over the mayonnaise and dill before serving.

Mussels with bacon & beer

I COOKED THIS DISH FOR THE FIRST TIME IN NAMIBIA WHEN I WAS FILMING AT SOSSUSVLEI GAME RESERVE, ON AN OPEN FIRE CALLED A BRAAI – A SORT OF OPEN BARBECUE. THE INGREDIENTS WERE SO SIMPLE BUT SUPERB, INCLUDING THE LARGEST MUSSELS I HAVE EVER SEEN. COUPLED WITH THE LOCAL LIGHT BEER, TAFEL, IT MADE A FANTASTIC LUNCH.

Serves 4   Preparation time 10 minutes   Cooking time 30 minutes

250g rindless smoked bacon, cut into 1cm cubes
1 large onion, finely chopped
1kg fresh cleaned mussels (chuck out any that refuse to close when firmly tapped)
350ml lager
salt and freshly ground black pepper

✱ Heat a large saucepan, add the cubed bacon and cook for 10 minutes, or until it is slightly browned and the fat is starting to run.

✱ Add the onion and cook for a further 10 minutes, again until it has taken on a nice colour.

✱ Add the mussels, a little salt and pepper and the beer and bring to a rapid boil. Stir well, cover and cook for 6–8 minutes, stirring occasionally, until all the mussels are open (throw out any that remain shut).

✱ Remove the pan from the hob, divide the mussels between four deep bowls and spoon over the lovely smoky beer liquor. I serve this with crusty bread.

Mini bacon
& sweetcorn fritters
with fresh tomato salsa

THIS IS GREAT, VERY EASY SNACK FOOD FOR BOTH KIDS AND ADULTS – MY KIDS LOVED THESE
FRITTERS WHEN THEY WERE GROWING UP. IT'S ALSO A GOOD WAY TO USE UP LEFTOVER BACON,
PORK OR EVEN HAM – REALLY ANYTHING GOES HERE. THIS RECIPE MAKES 10–12 SMALL FRITTERS.

Serves 4   Preparation time 20 minutes, plus standing   Cooking time 15 minutes

2 whole eggs, plus 1 egg white
100g plain flour, sifted
about 75ml milk
4–6 rindless smoked back bacon rashers
198g can sweetcorn kernels, drained
2 small shallots, finely chopped
pinch of ground cumin
1 tablespoon chopped fresh chives
vegetable oil, for frying
salt and freshly ground black pepper

SALSA
200g baby plum tomatoes, roughly chopped
½ red onion, finely chopped
2 tablespoons chopped fresh flat-leaf parsley
2 tablespoons olive oil

✱ Place the egg white in a large bowl and crack one of the whole eggs into another bowl. Separate the remaining whole egg and add the yolk to the bowl with the whole egg and the white to the other bowl containing the white.

✱ Add the flour and about 50ml of the milk to the whole egg and extra yolk and mix together – this should stop you getting a lumpy batter (says he!). Gradually beat in enough of the remaining milk to make a thick batter. Season well with salt and pepper and leave to stand for about 20 minutes.

✱ Meanwhile, grill the bacon on both sides until crisp. Leave to cool slightly, then cut into small pieces.

✱ For the salsa, mix all the salsa ingredients together in a bowl and season with salt and pepper.

✱ Tip the sweetcorn into a colander and use the back of a spoon to gently squeeze out any excess water. Add to the batter with the chopped shallots, bacon, cumin and chives.

✱ Whisk the egg whites until stiff, then add to the batter and fold together.

✱ Heat a little vegetable oil in a non-stick frying pan. Add separate spoonfuls of the batter mixture and allow them to spread slightly. Cook, in batches, over a medium heat for about 2–3 minutes, or until just set and golden brown on the base, then turn over and cook the other side.

✱ Serve the fritters hot with the fresh tomato salsa.

Hot bacon, roasted garlic & watercress salad

THIS SALAD MAY BE VERY SIMPLE, BUT IT'S ALSO VERY TASTY. THE SECRET IS TO HAVE EVERYTHING PREPARED BEFORE YOU BEGIN PUTTING IT TOGETHER – TRUST ME! DON'T BE ALARMED ABOUT THE AMOUNT OF GARLIC; ONCE COOKED IT WILL LOSE MOST OF ITS PUNGENCY. YOU CAN EITHER WHISK ALL THE DRESSING INGREDIENTS TOGETHER IN A BOWL OR PLACE THEM IN A CLEAN JAR, SCREW ON THE LID AND SHAKE WELL TO COMBINE. DON'T ADD THE DRESSING TO THE LEAVES UNTIL THE LAST MOMENT, OTHERWISE THEY WILL COLLAPSE AND WILT. TO EAT THE GARLIC CLOVES, JUST SQUEEZE THEM AND POP THE FLESH OUT OF THE SKINS.

Serves 4   Preparation time 20 minutes   Cooking time 20–25 minutes

2 heads of garlic
about 20 baby new potatoes, boiled and cooled
100g watercress
130g bag mixed green salad leaves
2 tablespoons vegetable oil
12 rindless streaky bacon rashers, cut into 2cm pieces
salt and freshly ground black pepper

DRESSING
3 tablespoons good-quality extra virgin olive oil
2 teaspoons Dijon or wholegrain mustard
pinch of caster sugar
juice of ½ lemon

✱ Break up the heads of garlic so that all the cloves are separate, then cut off the hard root of each, but don't remove too much of the clove.

✱ Put the cloves in their skins into a small saucepan of salted boiling water and bring back to the boil. Reduce the heat and simmer for 3–4 minutes, or until they are very soft, then drain.

✱ Cut the potatoes in half lengthways, and put the watercress and salad leaves in a large bowl.

✱ Heat the vegetable oil in a wok or large frying pan, add the bacon and cook slowly for 10–15 minutes, or until it starts to crisp up.

✱ Add the garlic (skins and all!) and potatoes and cook until they are all golden brown.

✱ Meanwhile, whisk the dressing ingredients together.

✱ Pour the dressing over the leaves and toss well. Pile equal amounts of the garlic, potato and bacon mixture onto plates, then pile the salad leaves on top. Serve straight away.

Baked potato, sweet cabbage & blue cheese layer cake

THIS IS A GREAT DISH, EASY TO PREPARE AND VERY TASTY. THE INGREDIENTS FORM THE BEDROCK OF IRISH FOOD, AND OVER THE CENTURIES THERE HAVE BEEN THOUSANDS OF RECIPES INVENTED USING THESE STAPLES. THE MELTING CHEESE COMBINES WITH THE COOKED POTATOES, BACON FAT AND CABBAGE TO MAKE A ONE-POT MEAL THAT IS SO SATISFYING.

Serves 4–6   Preparation time 20 minutes   Cooking time about 1 hour 15 minutes

25g unsalted butter
1 tablespoon olive oil
½ small Savoy cabbage, inner leaves only, very finely sliced
2 tablespoons vegetable oil, plus extra for oiling
200g streaky bacon, chopped
600g peeled medium potatoes, cut into 5mm-thick slices
150g blue cheese, such as Cashel Blue, roughly grated or chopped
salt and freshly ground black pepper

✱ Preheat the oven to 200°C/Gas 6.

✱ Heat the butter and olive oil together in a large sauté pan, add the cabbage and cook for about 15 minutes until softened. Drain well in a colander.

✱ Heat the vegetable oil in a frying pan, add the bacon and cook until the fat runs. Drain in a colander with the cabbage and reserve the fat.

✱ Toss the potato slices in the reserved bacon fat. Place a layer of them, overlapping, in the base of a lightly oiled 28cm non-stick ovenproof frying pan and season with a little salt and pepper. Spread over a little cabbage and bacon, then top with some of the cheese. This helps to keep the whole cake together. Continue overlapping and seasoning the potatoes, and layering with the cabbage, bacon and cheese.

✱ Place the pan on the hob and heat for a few seconds so that the potato starts to brown and bubble on the base.

✱ Cover lightly with foil and bake in the oven for about 50 minutes. Remove the foil and check whether the cake is cooked – you should be able to pierce it with a knife with no resistance. Replace the foil, then press down lightly to compact the cake.

✱ Leave to cool slightly, say 15 minutes, then turn out onto a chopping board, cut into wedges and serve with a few salad leaves dressed with a little French dressing.

CHAPTER 5 Sausages

According to Mark Twain, 'Those that respect the law and love sausages, should watch neither being made.' This quote has stuck in my mind for 20 years, and I refer to it with alarming regularity when discussing the humble sausage. I believe sausage making is an art form, and I have no issue at all with anyone looking at how mine are made. In fact, I would actively encourage people to come and watch the process, as I think it's important that everyone is aware of what they are eating, especially when supermarkets are trying their hardest to make our food as cheap as possible.

For me, sausages are a massively personal subject and a really important part of my business. My recipes are extremely precious too, and have taken years to perfect, so rather than write prescriptive recipes, what follows are the fundamentals, so that you can adapt them to make them your own.

For too long, British sausages were predominantly seen as an inexpensive way of feeding a family and a great way for butchers to use up meat scraps. This was never the philosophy adopted by our European counterparts. For them, the sausage has always been an important part of a butcher's repertoire, and the meat selection and quality control used in making them has left us trailing embarrassingly behind, in my opinion. However, with stricter food labelling and general food-quality awareness, we are at last catching up and even starting to produce some of the classics, such as bratwurst and Toulouse, to similar standards. As a rule, most European sausages contain only meat and water, or just meat, and therefore will have a much denser texture than the British banger. – Simon

Cooking sausages

COOKING SAUSAGES IS QUITE AN ART, AND IT
REALLY DEPENDS ON A FEW FACTORS AS TO WHICH
IS THE BEST WAY TO GO ABOUT IT. I WAS ONCE
TOLD BY ANOTHER CHEF THAT YOU MUST NEVER
PRICK A SAUSAGE; HE NEVER EXPLAINED WHY AND
I'M NOT SURE WHY HE WOULD SAY THAT. I HAVE
BEEN THINKING ABOUT IT FOR YEARS AND THE
ONLY VIABLE REASON COULD BE THAT IT STOPS
THEM EXPLODING.

✻ To my mind, there are four ways to cook a sausage: grilling,
baking, frying and barbecuing, essentially outdoor grilling. Some
sausages, like the French boudin blanc (white chicken sausage)
and boudin noir (blood sausage), are gently simmered. I prefer
to fry gently, then pop into a hot oven or under a hot grill,
turning occasionally to get a good all-round colour. This also
ensures they do not split, unless you overcook them. And whilst
we are on the subject, you must make sure you cook sausages
perfectly, as if under- or overcooked they are horrible.

✻ It goes without saying that the base product has to be of
good quality to start with. I have found that Simon's sausages
cook perfectly; this could be due to the fact that they have a
high percentage of meat, and of course fat, and even the right
amount of rusk to bind them. Too much rusk and they are dry,
too little and they fall apart. The skins make all the difference
when cooking a sausage and Simon only uses natural skins; it
has to help.

✻ One last point to highlight: NEVER deep-fry – this will
make your sausages look and taste disgusting! — Phil

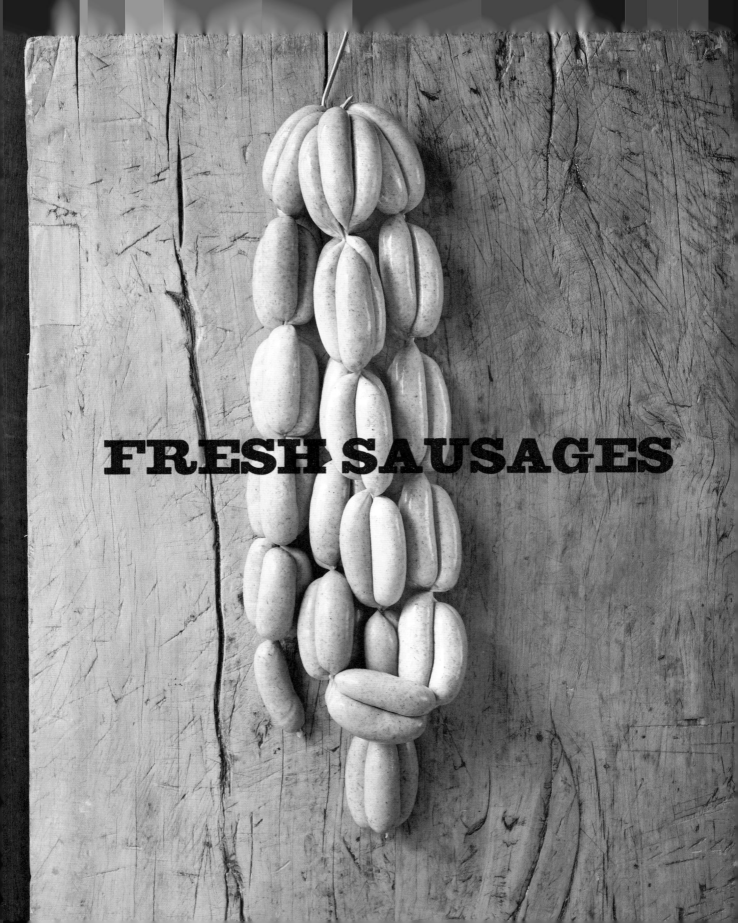

FRESH SAUSAGES

The British banger

THERE ARE THREE MAIN BUILDING BLOCKS TO A GOOD BANGER: TOP-QUALITY BELLY AND SHOULDER PORK (THE FAT CONTENT OF WHICH NEEDS TO BE 25 PER CENT); SEASONING (SALT AND GROUND WHITE PEPPER IS ALL YOU NEED TO START – FOR EVERY KILOGRAM OF MEAT YOU NEED 18G SALT AND 3G WHITE PEPPER); AND BINDER (BREAD RUSK IS MY PREFERRED CHOICE, 10 PER CENT OF THE TOTAL MIX IS PLENTY). THIS WILL MAKE A SUCCULENT PORK SAUSAGE WITH A WELL-ROUNDED FLAVOUR, BUT WITH THE ADDITION OF SPICES YOU CAN TAILOR-MAKE YOUR OWN SPECIALITY SAUSAGES. THE FOLLOWING RECIPE GIVES THE MOST COMMONLY USED SPICES AND QUANTITIES.

750g top-quality pork belly or shoulder (25% fat)
18g cooking salt
3g ground white pepper
100g bread rusk
150g chilled water
hog or sheep casings

PLUS ANY COMBINATION OF THE FOLLOWING, ACCORDING TO YOUR PREFERENCE:

2g dried sage
1g ground nutmeg
1g ground mace
0.5g ground ginger
2g dried thyme
2g paprika
1g dried chilli flakes
3g ground garlic
2g ground black pepper (coarsely ground is best)

✱ To my mind, the single most important factor in the production of sausages is how they are put together. Make sure the pork is extremely well chilled and trimmed free of gristle and sinew. Then mince through a coarse plate, i.e. one with holes of 10–13mm in diameter, into a large bowl.

✱ In a separate bowl, add the seasoning to the bread rusk and mix well. Pour in the water and leave until the rusk has absorbed it all.

✱ Add the soaked rusk mixture to the meat and mix thoroughly until nice and tacky.

✱ Re-mince the meat through a 5mm plate, then stuff the sausage meat into either hog or sheep casings and twist into 10–13cm links, or simply form into patties, then refrigerate for up to 2 days. You can also freeze them.

Pork with leek & stilton sausages

THIS IS A REALLY NICE, RUSTIC-LOOKING SAUSAGE, WHICH GIVES A WHOLE NEW MEANING TO A TOAD IN THE HOLE (SEE PAGE 141)!

Makes 1kg

750g pork shoulder
18g cooking salt
3g ground white pepper
100g bread rusk
150g chilled water
about ⅓ leek, washed well, sautéed until soft and cooled
50g Stilton cheese, crumbled
hog casings

✱ Mince the pork through an 8mm plate into a large bowl.

✱ In a separate bowl, add the seasoning to the bread rusk and mix well. Pour in the water and leave until the rusk has absorbed it all.

✱ Add the soaked rusk mixture to the meat along with the leek and Stilton, and mix thoroughly until nice and tacky.

✱ Stuff the sausage meat into hog casings and twist into 10–13cm links.

Pork with apricot & ginger sausages

ANOTHER RUSTIC-STYLE SAUSAGE, WHICH IS GREAT ON THE BARBECUE.

Makes 1kg

750g pork shoulder
18g cooking salt
3g ground white pepper
2g ground ginger
100g bread rusk
150g chilled water
50g ready-to-eat dried apricots, chopped
hog casings

Follow the method for the Pork with Leek & Stilton Sausages opposite, adding the ginger with the seasoning to the bread rusk and the chopped dried apricots to the meat with the soaked rusk mixture.

Cumberland sausage

THIS IS PERHAPS THE MOST POPULAR SAUSAGE IN THE UK AND THE MOST DISPUTED AS TO WHICH IS THE CORRECT RECIPE. THIS IS MY INTERPRETATION, BE IT RIGHT OR WRONG.

Makes 1kg

900g pork shoulder
18g cooking salt
3g ground white pepper
2g coarsely ground black pepper
2g English rubbed sage
50g bread rusk
50g chilled water
hog casings

Follow the method for the Pork with Leek & Stilton Sausages opposite, adding the sage with the seasoning to the bread rusk. Then after stuffing into hog casings, instead of twisting into links, leave in lengths to make coils.

Italian sausage

IT IS THE FENNEL SEEDS THAT MAKE THESE ITALIAN. THEY ARE ONE OF MY PERSONAL SAUSAGE FAVOURITES AND ARE DELICIOUS EITHER BARBECUED OR SIMMERED IN A SPICY TOMATO SAUCE.

Makes 1kg

1kg pork shoulder
18g cooking salt
3g cracked fennel seeds
2g ground white pepper
2g hot paprika
2g ground garlic
1g dried chilli flakes
hog casings

✱ Mince the pork through an 8mm plate into a large bowl – it is minced only once, but it's really important that there is no gristle at all.

✱ Combine all the dry ingredients and then mix with the minced meat thoroughly.

✱ Stuff the sausage meat into hog casings and twist into links, then refrigerate. They will keep in the fridge for a couple of days, but they also freeze well.

Bratwurst

BRATWURST IS A GENERIC NAME FOR ALL FRESH GERMAN SAUSAGES. THEY ARE TRADITIONALLY MADE WITH PORK AND VEAL, AND YOU WILL FIND EACH REGION IN GERMANY HAS ITS OWN STYLE, THURINGER AND NUREMBERG BEING TWO WELL-KNOWN EXAMPLES. THE MAJOR DIFFERENCE BETWEEN BRATWURST AND AN ENGLISH BANGER IS THAT BRATWURST DO NOT CONTAIN ANY BINDER, SUCH AS BREAD, WHICH GIVES BRATWURST A MUCH DENSER AND MEATIER TEXTURE. MY VERSION CONTAINS JUST PORK, AND THEY WORK REALLY WELL ON THE BARBECUE.

Makes 1kg

300g pork shoulder
600g pork belly
18g cooking salt
2g caster sugar
2g ground white pepper
1g ground nutmeg
1g ground ginger
1g dried marjoram
0.5g ground mace
100g chilled water
hog casings
butter, for pan-frying (optional)

✱ Mince the pork through a 5mm plate into a large bowl.

✱ Combine the dry ingredients with the chilled water, then mix into the meat until it is fully absorbed and the mixture is nice and tacky.

✱ Re-mince through the 5mm plate and give it another mix to ensure that it binds together.

✱ Stuff into hog casings and twist into links of the desired size.

✱ Refrigerate the sausages for at least 12 hours to allow the spices to diffuse through the meat.

✱ Poach in simmering water for about 25 minutes, then drain and pat dry with kitchen paper.

✱ When you are ready to eat, fry in a little butter in a frying pan until brown or cook on a barbecue or under a grill.

Nuremberg bratwurst

THIS IS THE ULTIMATE BRATWURST, DEMONSTRATING THE HIGH ART OF SAUSAGE MAKING. THERE IS NO ADDED WATER IN THIS SAUSAGE AND THE USE OF ONLY PORK COLLAR MAKES IT EXTREMELY HIGH QUALITY TOO. THEY ARE BEST EATEN BY THE DOZEN, WITH COPIOUS AMOUNTS OF GERMAN BEER!

Makes 1kg

1kg pork collar
18g cooking salt
2g ground white pepper
0.5g ground nutmeg
1g dried marjoram
1 egg, beaten (to help with binding)
sheep casings

✱ Mince the pork through a 5mm plate into a large bowl (it is minced only once).

✱ Combine all the seasonings, add to the meat with the egg and mix thoroughly until nice and tacky.

✱ Stuff the sausage meat into sheep casings, twist into links about 13cm long and refrigerate. I would always eat these the day after production. When you are ready to eat, fry in a little butter in a frying pan until brown.

Thüringer bratwurst

THURINGIAN SAUSAGES HAVE BEEN PRODUCED IN THE GERMAN STATE OF THURINGIA FOR HUNDREDS OF YEARS AND THERE ARE EVEN RECIPES DATING BACK TO 1613 STORED IN THE STATE ARCHIVES. MANY RECIPE VARIATIONS CAN BE FOUND THROUGHOUT THE REGION, BUT THEY ARE ALWAYS COOKED ON THE GRILL AND SERVED ON AN OPEN ROLL WITH KETCHUP AND MUSTARD (AND THE ODD BEER OR TWO).

Makes 1kg

700g pork shoulder
300g pork belly
18g cooking salt
2g ground white pepper
1g ground caraway seeds
1g dried marjoram
0.5g ground nutmeg
100g chilled water
hog casings

✱ Mince the pork through a 5mm plate into a large bowl (it is minced only once).

✱ Combine all the seasonings, add to the meat with the water and mix thoroughly until nice and tacky.

✱ Stuff the sausage meat into hog casings and twist into links about 15cm long.

✱ The sausages can be grilled as they are or poached first and then grilled – poaching first and then chilling straight away will increase their shelf life.

Christmas sausage rolls

I LIKE SAUSAGE ROLLS WHEN THEY ARE NOT SOGGY, FATTY AND UNDERCOOKED.
SO HERE IS A RECIPE YOU CAN DEPEND ON.

Makes 24   Preparation time 20 minutes, plus chilling   Cooking time 20–25 minutes

500g ready-rolled puff pastry
1 egg, beaten

FILLING
500g good-quality sausage meat, not too fatty (15–20 per cent is perfect)
150g ready-to-eat dried apricots, finely chopped
100g cooked peeled chestnuts, finely chopped
2 tablespoons chopped fresh sage

* Combine all the filling ingredients in a large bowl and mix together well.

* Place the sheets of pastry on a board and cut into 5cm-wide strips. Brush well with beaten egg.

* Using a piping bag, pipe the sausage meat onto the pastry strips, slightly to one side. Fold over and seal the edge well. Brush again with beaten egg, then chill well.

* When ready to cook, preheat the oven to 200°C/Gas 6.

* Cut the long rolls into 24 small rolls. Place on a baking tray and bake for 20–25 minutes until browned, crisp and cooked through.

Toad in the hole with posh onion gravy

THIS IS THE BEST TOAD IN THE HOLE RECIPE, THE SECRET BEING TO USE AN OVENPROOF FRYING PAN AND TO KEEP THE BATTER ONLY A COUPLE OF CENTIMETRES DEEP IN THE MIDDLE OF THE PAN. THIS WILL ENSURE A WELL-RISEN, CRISPY SIDE AND A COOKED BUT SLIGHTLY SOFT BOTTOM. ALSO, THE OVEN MUST BE HOT. I LIKE TO SERVE THIS WITH ONION GRAVY AND/OR A LARGE DOLLOP OF MUSTARD.

Serves 2   Preparation time 15 minutes   Cooking time about 45 minutes

115g plain flour
2 eggs, beaten
300ml milk
2 tablespoons olive oil
4 large sausages, spicy, Pork with Leek and Stilton (page 134) or Cumberland (page 135)
salt and ground white pepper

GRAVY (serves 4–6)
2 tablespoons olive oil
3 large onions, finely sliced
2 glasses red wine
1 teaspoon fresh thyme, chopped
1 tablespoon plain flour
1.2 litres good strong beef stock
2 tablespoons redcurrant jelly
salt and freshly ground black pepper

✽ Preheat the oven to 220°C/Gas 7.

✽ For the gravy, heat the olive oil in a saucepan, add the onions and cook for 15 minutes to soften. Add the wine and thyme and cook down until almost evaporated. Stir in the flour and mix well, then blend in the stock and redcurrant jelly and cook gently for 20 minutes, or until thickened. Season well with salt and black pepper.

✽ While the gravy is cooking, make the toad in the hole. Sift the flour into a large bowl, make a well in the centre and add the eggs and half the milk to the well. Whisk slowly, gradually incorporating the flour from the edge of the bowl. Add the remaining milk and whisk well until smooth, then season with salt and white pepper. Leave to stand while you cook the sausages.

✽ Heat the olive oil in a 25cm non-stick, ovenproof frying pan. Add the sausages and brown nicely all over. Pour the batter into the hot sausage pan and then quickly transfer to the hot oven. Immediately reduce the temperature to 200°C/Gas 6.

✽ Cook for 25–35 minutes, or until well risen and golden around the edge. Remove from the oven and eat straight away with the hot onion gravy.

Spicy sausages braised in red onion marmalade

THIS IS ANOTHER NICE AND VERY EASY WAY OF COOKING SAUSAGES, AND IT'S VERY SATISFYING. IT JUST HAS TO BE SERVED WITH MASHED POTATOES.

Serves 4   Preparation time 10 minutes   Cooking time 30 minutes

2 tablespoons vegetable oil
8 Cumberland sausage pieces, about 100g each (page 135)
6 red onions, very finely sliced
2 tablespoons soft dark brown sugar
2 tablespoons Worcestershire sauce
1 large glass red wine
2 tablespoons malt vinegar
salt and freshly ground black pepper

✱ Heat the vegetable oil in a large frying pan with a lid and brown the sausage pieces all over, then remove from the pan and set aside.

✱ Add the onions and brown well, then add all the remaining ingredients with a little salt and pepper.

✱ Cover and cook gently for about 20 minutes, or until the onions are soft. Remove the lid, return the sausages to the pan and cook, uncovered, for a further 10 minutes, or until the sauce is thick and syrupy, and coating the sausages really well. Serve with mash.

CURED SAUSAGES

These are sausages made with meat that has been cured with salt and sodium nitrite. Cured sausages can be fermented and dried like salami and chorizo, emulsified like hot dogs and frankfurters, or simply coarsely ground and smoked like polish kielbasa.

My fascination with this subject began shortly after I bought my butchery business. At the time I didn't realise how popular cured sausages were around the world, or that they would grow hugely in popularity here in the UK. Over the years I have tried hundreds of different recipes but these are mostly my first dalliances with cured sausages and remain my favourites. – Simon

Reddening is the fermentation process. When the sausages are first made, they will turn a horrible grey colour. After 12–14 hours, however, the salt, sugars and starter cultures will have started to work, and the sausages will become a lovely red colour.

Tempering is when frozen meat is placed in a cold fridge running at 0–2°C and left to temper/defrost until it reaches a temperature of approximately 2°C.

Andouille

THIS IS MY VERSION OF THE CLASSIC LOUISIANA SMOKED SAUSAGE, WHICH IS USUALLY SEEN IN DISHES LIKE JAMBALAYA AND GUMBO. BUT I LOVE THEM SIMPLY DONE ON THE BARBECUE WITH A NICE HONEY AND MUSTARD GLAZE.

Makes 1kg

1kg pork shoulder (completely trimmed of gristle and sinew)
18g curing salt (containing 0.6% sodium nitrite)
4g coarsely ground black pepper
2g chilli powder
8g finely chopped garlic (about 2 cloves)
100g chilled water
hog casings

* Mince the pork through a 5mm plate into a large bowl.

* Combine the dry ingredients and then mix into the minced meat with the garlic and water until thoroughly combined.

* Stuff the sausage meat into hog casings and twist into 10–13cm links.

* Leave the sausages to dry at room temperature for an hour or so and then hot smoke at 76°C until a core temperature of 68°C is reached.

Brickhill smokies

THIS WAS THE FIRST SMOKED SAUSAGE I MADE, INSPIRED BY READING THE BIOGRAPHY OF A POLISH SAUSAGE MAKER IN THE USA. I HAVE ADDED ONE OR TWO MORE INGREDIENTS TO MAKE IT MY OWN.

Makes 1kg

1kg pork shoulder or butt, tempered (see page 144)
18g curing salt (0.6% sodium nitrite)
10g ground garlic
2g ground white pepper
1g hot chilli powder
50g runny honey
hog casings

✱ Mince the pork through an 8mm plate into a large bowl (it is minced only once).

✱ Mix the minced meat with the curing salt, seasonings and honey thoroughly until it becomes really sticky and tacky.

✱ Stuff the sausage meat into hog casings, twist into links and refrigerate overnight to allow the spices to diffuse through the meat.

✱ Hang the sausages in a smoker until they reach room temperature and the skins are dry, then apply smoke until the desired colour is obtained (see opposite).

✱ Simmer or steam the sausages at 80°C until an internal temperature of 70°C is reached for at least 2 minutes.

✱ Hang the sausages in the fridge for 3 hours to cool. Alternatively, you can hang them in a cool, airy place to air dry for a week, which really intensifies the flavour and also prolongs the shelf life.

SALAMI

Raw, fermented salami has been produced around the world for hundreds of years and is considered to be an art form. It was the knowledge and expertise passed down through generations that traditionally ensured that quality products were produced. Today, however, with regulation and constant food-safety awareness, modern technology plays a big part in salami production, though we still need the expertise!

Salami manufacture consists of three stages:

1. Production & stuffing

Selecting the appropriate meat is paramount when producing salamis. I prefer to use shoulder muscles from a mature female pig that have been trimmed of all soft fat and gristle, so that you have virtually 100 per cent lean meat, and the hard back fat that is found on the neck of the pig. The ratio is usually 85 per cent lean meat to 15 per cent fat. The meat and fat are frozen and then left to temper in the fridge until it reaches a temperature of -2°C (see page 144). I prefer to mince the meat through an 8mm plate on the mincer and mix in the curing ingredients by hand, as this gives the final product a lovely rustic homemade look that is so desired these days (especially by Phil). The salami can then be stuffed into the casings. I use ox runners (part of the bovine large intestine) because they are not too wide and, being natural, will dry uniformly and relatively quickly to give that true artisan look.

2. Fermentation

This is the process by which the predominantly raw sausage is turned into a microbiologically- and shelf-stable product. Starter cultures are added to the mix before being stuffed into casings, and the stuffed salami is then subjected to temperatures of 22–26°C and a relative humidity of 90–93 per cent for a period of 12–16 hours. This encourages the cultures to grow and produce lactic acid, which together with the presence of sodium nitrite in the curing salt, helps to drop the water activity and pH value of the salami and in turn contribute to its microbiological stability. If the fermentation process has worked correctly, the salamis will have turned a lovely red colour and will be slightly firm to the touch. However, if you are making salamis to sell, investing in a pH meter is the only way to verify that this process has occurred – they should exhibit a pH of around 5 if they have fermented properly.

3. Drying & maturation

This is the stage during which we want the salami to lose a certain amount of moisture in a relatively short period of time without drying too quickly around the outside and hardening the case. As a rule of thumb, this process is usually achieved at a temperature of 12–15°C and a relative humidity of 72–78 per cent with a minimal amount of airflow (zero airflow will encourage the growth of mould). Ideally, you are looking for a weight loss of approximately 30 per cent before the salamis will be ready.

'Twiggies'

THESE SNACK SALAMIS WERE THE PRODUCT OF MY FIRST VENTURE INTO SALAMI MAKING. ONCE I HAD FINISHED MAKING THEM I REMEMBER THINKING THAT THEY WOULD NEVER REDDEN UP, BUT THEY DID AND I WAS HOOKED! A STARTER CULTURE (SEE PAGE 199) IS CRUCIAL TO THE FERMENTATION OF SALAMI. IT CONSISTS OF SELECTED BACTERIA THAT FERMENT SUGARS AND PRODUCE LACTIC ACID, PROVIDING THE PRONOUNCED SALAMI FLAVOUR AND ALSO AIDING COLOUR DEVELOPMENT AND THE MICROBIOLOGICAL STABILITY OF THE FINAL PRODUCT.

Makes 1kg (10–12 sausages)

750g pork shoulder, tempered (see page 144)
250g pork belly, tempered (see page 144)
26g curing salt (containing 0.6% sodium nitrite)
3g ground white pepper
3g glucose
2g sodium ascorbate
0.5 g starter culture (see Glossary, page 199)
sheep casings

✻ Mince the tempered pork through a 5mm plate into a large bowl (it is minced only once).

✻ Combine all the dry ingredients and mix thoroughly with the pork.

✻ Stuff the sausage meat into sheep casings and twist into links.

✻ Hang the sausages in a warm, humid environment at a temperature of about 25°C for about 12 hours – an airing cupboard with some damp towels is ideal. During this time the sausages will redden and begin to dry.

✻ Next, move the sausages to an environment with a temperature of 12–15°C and a humidity of about 78 per cent with little airflow – a cellar or pantry would work well. They should be ready to eat in about 10 days.

Snack chorizos

THIS IS A WONDERFUL VERSION OF THE SPANISH CLASSIC. THE SAUSAGES ARE MADE IN EXACTLY THE SAME WAY AS THE TWIGGIES BUT WITH SWEET, SMOKED AND HOT PAPRIKA AND GROUND GARLIC ADDED TO THE SEASONINGS – SEE BELOW FOR THE COMPLETE LIST OF INGREDIENTS.

Makes 1kg

750g pork shoulder, tempered (see page 144)
250g pork belly, tempered (see page 144)
26g curing salt (containing 0.6% sodium nitrite)
10g smoked paprika
7g hot paprika
3g ground white pepper
3g sweet paprika

3g glucose
2g ground garlic
2g sodium ascorbate
0.5g starter culture (see Glossary, page 199)
sheep casings

Follow the method for 'Twiggies' above.

Hot dogs

THESE 'DOGS' ARE INSPIRED BY THE CLASSIC GERMAN FRANKFURTER. I HAVE TWEAKED THE SEASONING AND TEXTURE OF THE SAUSAGE MEAT A LITTLE TO CALL IT MY OWN. TO MAKE CHEESY DOGS, USE THE SAME INGREDIENTS AS BELOW BUT ADD 100G FINELY DICED CHEDDAR TO THE MIX WITH THE DRY INGREDIENTS, AND FOLLOW THE SAME METHOD.

Makes 1kg

500g pork butt/shoulder
300g pork belly
18g curing salt (0.6% sodium nitrite)
2g ground white pepper
2g paprika
1g ground garlic
1g ground nutmeg
1g ground mace
0.5g ground ginger
0.5g chilli powder

✱ Mince the pork through an 8mm plate into a large bowl.

✱ Combine the dry ingredients and mix into the meat, slowly adding the water until the mixture is really sticky and tacky.

✱ Re-mince the mixture through a 5mm plate.

✱ Stuff the sausage meat into hog casings and twist into links, then smoke as for the Brickhill Smokies and simmer or steam (see page 146).

HOT DOG SERVINGS

Serving hot dogs really is a very personal thing. I tend to stick to the basic staples and never really stray away, I suppose I'm a bit of a traditionalist. So that means sautéed onions, long and slow with a little salt pepper and sugar. Next, yellow mustard – the type that comes in the squeezy bottle. Ketchup? Yes, but not too much. Finally, slab cheese. Yes, love it or hate it – partially melted is the only way. The only real exception is when I'm in America. Then I will sometimes have a chilli dog: chilli ground beef on top of my hot dog – its a bit difficult to eat but lovely!

Sausage, chorizo and bean casserole

THIS IS SO SIMPLE TO MAKE BUT PACKED FULL OF VEGETABLES AND FLAVOUR. ANY SAUSAGE WILL DO, BUT THE ADDITION OF THE CHORIZO GIVES THE DISH A REAL KICK OF COLOUR AND FLAVOUR.

Serves 4   Preparation time 20 minutes   Cooking time about 50 minutes

2 tablespoons oil (any type will do)
400g prime pork bangers
200g chorizo, skin removed and cut into 2.5mm slices
2 tablespoons tomato purée
2 red onions, sliced
2 garlic cloves, chopped
2 red peppers, deseeded and roughly chopped
2 celery sticks, roughly chopped
400g can tomatoes
400g can red kidney beans, well rinsed
2 tablespoons vinegar
2 tablespoons soft brown sugar
3 bay leaves
about 300ml strong chicken stock
2 tablespoons cornflour

✱ Preheat the oven to 200°C/Gas 6.

✱ Heat the oil in a large ovenproof pan with a lid, add the sausages and brown well. Add the chorizo and tomato purée and mix well.

✱ Add all the remaining ingredients except the cornflour and mix together thoroughly. Cover and cook in the oven for 35–40 minutes.

✱ Remove the dish from the oven and uncover. Bring to a gentle simmer on the hob. Blend the cornflour with a little cold water, then stir into the dish and cook, stirring, until thickened. Serve with mash.

CHAPTER 6 Odd bits

Many years ago, the 'odd bits', as I call them, were used all the time. Every part of the pig was consumed in some way, shape or form, apart from the toe nails and the squeak! In my very first cookbook, given to me in the early 1970s, I have two recipes handwritten by me. The first is for my dad's favourite pudding of all time, bread pudding. The second is a recipe for brawn, or head cheese as the French like to call it. I vividly remember my dad boiling this huge pig's head, with onions and peppercorns, then cooling and removing all the bits of flesh, cartilage, brain and tongue. Everything would be carefully chopped with onions and the stock reduced, then packed into a clear Pyrex bowl and chilled. My mother hated it, but my dad, my brothers and I all loved it; in fact, I still love it to this day.

So when it comes to cooking extremities and other odd bits I am very at home, though they really aren't Simon's cup of tea. This is probably where butchers and chefs don't see eye to eye. We have had many a conversation as to why he hates offal, and we never agree. From my point of view, with some careful thought and a bit of prep, all these bits and bobs can be really tasty.

Let's start from the front, with snout. Okay, it's not often used, but with simple preparation and cooking it can be turned into something quite delicious. Layered with potato, onions, bacon and stock, cooked really slowly, the soft cartilage melting into a truly great dish.

Even my 12-year-old daughter likes it.

With the outbreak of BSE, brain, admittedly never hugely popular, disappeared off the menu but it is now making a comeback. I love it gently poached, then coated in a light batter and fried – its creamy texture works perfectly with crunchy ingredients such as raw vegetables or Iceberg lettuce. Cheeks, on the other hand, are very trendy now. This small nut of meat braises beautifully with cider and onions, but can also be cured, pancetta style, and thinly sliced, eaten raw or lightly sautéed. Ears have always been a favourite of mine; twice cooked, Chinese style, they have a great texture and gelatinous mouth feel. I once had them on my menu as an intercourse, and they went down a storm, partly because I didn't charge for them – just a nice thing to do, I thought. After that, they became a staple. The same careful treatment of tongues, hearts, liver and kidneys also pays huge dividends.

Which brings me, finally, to scratchings or crackling. Yes, out of all the recipes in the book, this is the one that took the longest to get right. It takes a few hours to prepare, and some (Simon included) might think it's a lot of effort to go to for a bit of old pork skin, but for the hardcore of people who enjoy this most comforting of foods, it very definitely is worth it. I LOVE IT! Drizzled with a little malt vinegar and sprinkled with salt, or dipped into a bowl of sharp apple compôte there is nothing else to eat with a glass of chilled dry cider. – Phil

Pressed tongue in parsley peppercorn jelly

TONGUE IS NOT EVERYONE'S CUP OF TEA I KNOW, BUT TO ME IT'S ONE OF THE BEST PARTS OF THE PIG. PIG'S TONGUES ARE A THIRD OF THE SIZE OF AN OX TONGUE, BUT WITH A FINER TEXTURE AND FLAVOUR. WHEN I WAS COOKING PROFESSIONALLY, WE WOULD COOK 4-6 OX TONGUES PER WEEK AND THEY ALWAYS WENT DOWN WELL AT LUNCHTIME. WE WOULD MAKE A SHARP GHERKIN SAUCE FINISHED WITH A DASH OF CREAM TO SERVE WITH IT, SLICED OVER MASHED POTATOES. A MORE REFINED VERSION CONSISTED OF THE TONGUE FINELY SLICED WITH A LIGHT MADEIRA SAUCE ALONG WITH PEELED GRAPES AND TOASTED FLAKED ALMONDS. I EVEN ENCOUNTERED A LADY WHO WANTED THE GRAPE VERSION FOR HER DOG'S DINNER! HERE, PIG TONGUE IS SIMPLY COOKED AND SET IN A JELLY TO GRACE THE LUNCH OR TEATIME TABLE.

Serves 6-8   Preparation time 15 minutes, plus 4-5 days' curing, then chilling   Cooking time about 2 hours 15 minutes

4 large pig's tongues, washed well
1 trotter, cleaned and washed really well
2 carrots, peeled but left whole
2 onions, peeled but left whole
2 celery sticks
1 small leek, trimmed and washed but left whole
4 tablespoons vinegar
a few black peppercorns, plus a few extra
a few fresh parsley stalks, plus a few extra leaves
4 bay leaves
salt and freshly ground black pepper

CURE
1 litre water
120g curing salt (containing 0.6% sodium nitrite)

✱ To cure the tongues and trotter, put the water and curing salt into a large plastic or stainless steel bowl or container and mix well – the easiest way is to use warm water and then chill the cure. Add the tongues and trotter and mix really thoroughly. Make sure they are covered with the water – I use a saucer to keep them submerged.

✱ Leave in the refrigerator for 4-5 days, turning the tongues occasionally.

✱ Wash the cured tongues and trotter really well in plenty of fresh cold water.

✱ Put the cured tongues and trotter into a saucepan and add all the remaining ingredients except the extra peppercorns and parsley leaves. Bring to the boil, then reduce the heat and simmer gently for about 2 hours, or until a skewer can pass through the thickest part of the meat with little resistance.

✱ Once the tongues are cooked, use rubber gloves to remove them from the cooking liquor. Carefully peel the skin from the hot tongues with your fingers – you must do this while they are still hot, or the skin won't come off.

✱ Remove the trotter and keep for another recipe, such as the Twice-cooked Trotters with Mango Chutney Glaze on page 165 (my dad would love to chew on it just as it is). Discard the vegetables and then gently simmer the cooking liquor for about 10 minutes until it is reduced by half, tasting to check that it's not too salty. This will ensure that the jelly from the trotter will set perfectly.

✱ Put the tongues into a small bowl and pack in well. Season the reduced stock, add the extra peppercorns and a few parsley leaves and then pour over the tongues. Chill well until set.

✱ Serve sliced with crusty bread and a few pickles such as gherkins, capers and a little roasted garlic mayonnaise. The jelly will be delicious and so will the tongue.

Tail soup with jumbo couscous & cabbage

JUMBO OR ISRAELI COUSCOUS IS SOMETHING I DISCOVERED MANY YEARS AGO WHEN I WAS IN THE USA. THE GRANULE IS LARGE, WITH AN ALMOST PEARL-LIKE SHAPE AND HAS A DELICIOUS TEXTURE WHEN COOKED. IT MAKES A NICE CHANGE FROM THE STANDARD VARIETY OF COUSCOUS AND WORKS REALLY WELL IN SOUPS AND STEWS.

Serves 4   Preparation time 30 minutes   Cooking time 2 hours 30 minutes

10 pig's tails
1 pork hock, fresh, smoked or brined (see page 85)
2 large carrots, peeled and chopped into medium-sized pieces
2 celery sticks, chopped into medium-sized pieces
2 large onions, chopped into medium-sized pieces
1 leek, trimmed, washed well and chopped into medium-sized pieces
2 bay leaves
1 teaspoon black peppercorns
a pinch or two of salt
100g jumbo or Israeli couscous
2 x 10g chicken stock cubes, crumbled
½ small white cabbage, finely sliced

✻ Remove any hairs from the tails by using a kitchen blowtorch or holding over a gas flame with tongs. Then wash the tails and the hock well.

✻ Put the tails and hock into a large saucepan, cover with cold water and bring to the boil. Then reduce the heat and simmer gently for 5 minutes, skimming off any scum.

✻ If using brined hocks, taste the water and replace with fresh water if it is too salty. Then add all the vegetables, bay leaves, peppercorns, a little salt, couscous and stock cubes, and return to the boil.

✻ Reduce the heat and cook gently for 2 hours 15 minutes, or until the hock is cooked and you can remove the second smaller bone (the larger bone should stay in the joint). You may have to top up the pan with boiling water every so often. The water should be gently simmering; if the hock cooks too quickly, the outside meat will become really dry and stringy before the centre is cooked.

✻ Once cooked, remove the tails and hocks and leave to cool slightly. Meanwhile, add the cabbage to the pan and bring to the boil, then simmer for 5 minutes.

✻ Remove the fat and skin from the hock, then roughly chop the meat and add to the soup. Do the same with the tails.

✻ Return to the boil and taste – the soup should be like a minestrone or ribollita in consistency, i.e. nice and thick with veg, meat and couscous. Serve the soup in deep bowls with crusty bread.

Twice-cooked trotters with mango chutney glaze

TROTTERS ARE QUITE IN VOGUE NOW IN THE UK, BUT THEY ARE ALSO USED EXTENSIVELY IN THE FAR EAST, ITALY AND EVEN SPAIN. MY FATHER ALWAYS LOVED THEM BOILED WITH VINEGAR AND SALT AND PEPPER. TO ME THERE IS SOMETHING QUITE COMFORTING IN THE LOVELY JELLY AND SOFT TEXTURE OF THE TENDONS AND MEAT. WHICHEVER RECIPE YOU USE, YOU WILL NEED TO COOK THEM RIGHT THROUGH FIRST. SIMMERING WORKS FINE, AND SO DOES BAKING THEM IN A LOW OVEN. I USE BOTH METHODS; IT'S REALLY UP TO YOU. THIS DOES TAKE A COUPLE OF HOURS, BUT IT'S WELL WORTH THE WAIT. THE MANGO GLAZE IS A PERFECT FOIL FOR THE RICH MEAT. SERVE JUST AS THEY COME TO EAT WITH YOUR FINGERS.

Serves 4   Preparation time 25 minutes, plus soaking, cooling/chilling   Cooking time about 3 hours in total

4 large trotters, washed well
500ml good-quality chicken or pork stock, or 500ml water and 2 x 10g chicken or pork stock cubes, crumbled
2 large onions, peeled and cut into wedges
a few sprigs of fresh thyme
1 head of garlic, sliced in half horizontally
salt and freshly ground black pepper

GLAZE
225g mango chutney or any other sweet fruit chutney or relish
2 tablespoons tomato purée
2 tablespoons cider vinegar
1 small red chilli, finely chopped
4 garlic cloves, finely chopped
4 tablespoons olive oil

✱ Soak the trotters in cold water for a couple of hours. Then preheat the oven to 180°C/Gas 4.

✱ Place a deep, ovenproof pan with a tight-fitting lid on the hob and add the drained trotters. Add the stock or water and stock cubes, onions, thyme, salt and pepper and garlic, and bring to the boil. Leave for 2 minutes, then cover.

✱ Transfer to the oven and cook for 1 hour 30 minutes. At this point, remove from the oven and gently turn the trotters over; they will probably have started to split due to the tendons contracting. Re-cover and return to the oven for a further hour, maybe slightly longer, until soft and squidgy.

✱ Once cooked, leave to cool and then chill well.

✱ When ready to re-cook, remove the trotters from the jelly (keep the jelly to form a fabulous soup base, perhaps for the Tail Soup with Jumbo Couscous & Cabbage on page 162) and place in a small roasting tray large enough to accommodate all four trotters with a few centimetres' gap between them.

✱ Preheat the oven to 200°C/Gas 6.

✱ Make up the glaze by whisking all the ingredients together, then spoon over the trotters. Cook in the hot oven for 15–20 minutes, by which time they will be glazing nicely, although you will probably find that the glaze may go slightly runny at the start, as some of the jelly will ooze out of the trotters. Turn the trotters over and reglaze with a spoon until all the glaze has stuck to the trotters.

✱ When deeply glazed, remove from the oven and leave to cool for 10 minutes, then tuck in. No knives and forks, just fingers and bibs!

Warm liver parfait with crunchy rye topping

THIS IS A SIMPLE PARFAIT, OR VERY FINE MOUSSE, THAT WORKS WELL WITH ALL LIVERS. THE SECRET IS TO ACHIEVE AS SMOOTH A PURÉE AS POSSIBLE AT ROOM TEMPERATURE SO THAT WHEN YOU ADD THE WARM BUTTER IT WILL HOMOGENISE PERFECTLY. IF THE LIVER IS TOO COLD, AS IN STRAIGHT FROM THE FRIDGE, THE WARM BUTTER WILL SET IMMEDIATELY, GIVING YOU A SPLIT EFFECT RATHER THAN A PERFECTLY SMOOTH END RESULT.

Serves 4   Preparation time 20 minutes, plus cooling   Cooking time about 1 hour

250g fresh rye bread, cut into cubes
200ml port
200ml chicken stock
400g pig's liver, without tubes and skin, at room temperature, chopped
1 egg
350g unsalted butter, melted and warm but not hot
salt and ground white pepper

✱ Preheat the oven to 160°C/Gas 3.

✱ Place the rye bread in a food-processor and process into fine crumbs – you are not looking for dust, just a rough, even crumb similar to a crumble topping.

✱ Spread out the breadcrumbs on a baking tray and place in the oven to dry thoroughly until crunchy – this should take 20–25 minutes, stirring occasionally. Leave to cool.

✱ Meanwhile, pour the port and stock into a saucepan and bring to the boil, then cook over a medium heat until reduced by three-quarters. Leave to cool.

✱ Put the liver into a blender along with the cooled port and stock mixture and blitz until really smooth. Add the egg and pour in the melted butter on a medium speed (too much speed and for too long will make the parfait too light and moussey, and it will rise like a soufflé and also collapse like one).

✱ Strain the mousse through a sieve and season well with salt and white pepper.

✱ Mix well and then pour into four individual ramekins. Cover each one with a small piece of foil, then place in a deep baking tray. Fill the tray half full with boiling water and carefully transfer to the oven. Cook for 35–40 minutes, or until the parfait is just wobbly and set; do not overcook.

✱ Remove from the oven and lift the ramekins out of the water with a cloth. Leave to set for 5 minutes, then sprinkle over a nice topping of the rye breadcrumbs and serve straight away.

✱ This parfait also works well cold pâté style with Melba toast.

Pâté

A PRODUCT THAT IS MADE WORLDWIDE, PÂTÉ IS A BIT LIKE MARMITE – YOU EITHER LOVE IT OR HATE IT. THE PREDOMINANT INGREDIENT IS USUALLY LIVER AND MY VIEW IS THAT MOST OF THE COMMERCIALLY AVAILABLE PÂTÉS CONTAIN FAR TOO MUCH OF IT (PROBABLY BECAUSE IT COSTS NEXT TO NOTHING). MY FAVOURITE SORT IS AN INTERPRETATION OF A GERMAN COUNTRY PÂTÉ CALLED BAUERNLEBERWURST (FARMER'S LIVER SAUSAGE).

Makes 1kg

700g fatty pork belly, cooked and still hot – I usually cook the meat
    in an oven bag to retain all the cooking juices for the pâté
300g pig's liver, without tubes and skin
18g curing salt (containing 0.6% sodium nitrite)
3g fee (emulsifying agent – see Glossary, page 198)
20g gutsleberwurst (liver sausage seasoning, available from good butchers)
2 eggs, beaten
ox bungs (bovine large intestine), optional

✱ Mince the cooked belly and liver through a 5mm plate into a large bowl. Add the cooking juices and all the other ingredients, except the ox bungs, and mix very thoroughly.

✱ Dispense into foil trays or terrines and wrap tightly in clingfilm or foil. Then steam cook at 80°C until an internal temperature of 70°C is reached.

✱ I sometimes stuff the pâté into ox bungs and smoke it for about 30 minutes before I cook it, which gives it a really rustic look and a wonderful flavour.

Sherried kidneys

I LOVE KIDNEYS – MY DAD ALWAYS BOUGHT PORK CHOPS WITH THE KIDNEY STILL ATTACHED. THIS IS A VERY EASY DISH THAT MATCHES THE NOBLE PIG'S KIDNEY WITH A LITTLE SHERRY OR MADEIRA. TAKE CARE NOT TO OVERCOOK THE KIDNEYS OR THEY WILL BECOME DRY; IN FACT, LEAVING THEM A LITTLE PINK IS DELICIOUS.

Serves 4   Preparation time 15 minutes   Cooking time 20–25 minutes

30g unsalted butter
1 onion, very finely chopped
2 teaspoons Dijon mustard
2 large pig's kidneys, skinned and cut into 2cm pieces
1 tablespoon plain flour
175ml or large glass dry sherry or Madeira
200ml any meat stock or gravy
salt and freshly ground black pepper
3 tablespoons chopped fresh flat-leaf parsley, to serve

✱ Heat the butter in a sauté pan until just foaming, then add the onion and cook for 3–4 minutes to soften slightly. Then add the mustard and cook for a further 5 minutes.

✱ Add the kidneys and flour and mix well, then cook until the kidneys start to change colour. Stir in the sherry or Madeira and stock or gravy and season with a little salt and pepper.

✱ Reduce the heat and gently simmer for 10 minutes; no more, or the kidneys will dry out too much. Adjust the seasoning and serve with lots of chopped parsley.

✱ This makes a nice starter, or a main course with steamed rice or even mashed potatoes.

Sautéed kidneys with green sauce

THE SECRET WITH KIDNEYS IS TO AVOID OVERCOOKING THEM. ONCE GRILLED, BARBECUED OR SAUTÉED UNTIL STILL PINK, LEAVE THEM TO STAND FOR 5–10 MINUTES AND THEY WILL BE PERFECT. THIS GREEN SAUCE IS MORE OF A PUNCHY, CHLOROPHYLL-PACKED SEASONING, WHICH COMPLEMENTS THE KIDNEY REALLY WELL. I SOMETIMES ADD A FEW ANCHOVY FILLETS OR EVEN A LITTLE FRESH GREEN CHILLI TO THE OTHER INGREDIENTS FOR THE SAUCE, TO LIVEN IT UP EVEN FURTHER.

Serves 4   Preparation time 15 minutes   Cooking time 10 minutes at the most

4 tablespoons olive oil
15g unsalted butter
4 pig's kidneys, skinned and cut in half horizontally, but not completely through
2–3 tablespoons plain flour
500g thin asparagus spears, trimmed

SAUCE
150–200ml extra virgin olive oil
2 fresh garlic cloves, peeled
2 tablespoons drained capers
salt and freshly ground black pepper
25g fresh basil
25g fresh flat-leaf parsley
50g fresh spinach

✱ Heat a large frying pan on the hob and add the olive oil and butter.

✱ Open the kidneys up and flatten so that you have a large double kidney but with the halves still attached to each other.

✱ Once the butter is foaming and changing colour slightly, dust the kidneys in a little flour on both sides and add to the oil and butter. (Flouring not only gives a nice edge to the end dish but also reduces the amount of spitting from the pan.) Cook for 2–3 minutes, then turn over and cook for a further 2–3 minutes; do not overcook. Remove from the pan and leave to rest.

✱ Add the asparagus to the pan and cook for a couple of minutes to take on a little colour.

✱ Meanwhile, for the sauce, pour 150ml olive oil into a blender and add the garlic, capers, salt and a little pepper. Blitz until smooth, then add the herbs and spinach and blitz again, adding the extra oil if needed to get a really thick green sauce. Spoon into a bowl and adjust the seasoning if necessary.

✱ Serve each kidney with a few asparagus spears and a good spoonful of the sauce – simple and delicious.

Simple kidney stew with baby apple dumplings

I LOVE DUMPLINGS IN ANY SHAPE OR FORM, AND I ESPECIALLY LIKE CRUNCHY-TOPPED ONES. HERE, TART COOKING APPLE, VERY FINELY CHOPPED OR GRATED, IS NEEDED TO CUT THE RICHNESS NOT ONLY OF THE KIDNEY BUT ALSO THE SUET, AND TO MAKE THE DUMPLINGS LIGHT AND FLUFFY. THIS IS A PERFECT WINTER STARTER FOR FOUR OR A HEFTY MAIN WITH MASHED POTATOES.

Serves 4   Preparation time 25 minutes   Cooking time 35 minutes

2 tablespoons olive oil
1 red onion, peeled and sliced into wedges
2 garlic cloves, crushed
350g (2 medium) pig's kidneys, skinned and cut into 2cm pieces
1 tablespoon plain flour
about 500ml strong chicken or beef stock

DUMPLINGS
125g self-raising flour
65g suet
1 very small tart cooking apple, such as a Bramley,
   peeled, cored and very finely chopped or grated
1 egg, beaten
about 2 tablespoons water
salt and freshly ground black pepper

✱ Preheat the oven to 200°C/Gas 6.

✱ Heat the olive oil in a shallow ovenproof saucepan, roughly 30cm in diameter; there is a reason for this that I will explain later. Add the onion and garlic and cook for 3-4 minutes so that the onion takes on a little colour. Next, add the kidney and stir until it also takes on a little colour.

✱ Add the flour and mix well, then add enough stock to cover the kidneys plus another 1cm. Bring to the boil and then turn off the heat.

✱ Now make the dumplings. Put the flour, suet and salt and pepper into a bowl and mix well. Add the apple, beaten egg and water and mix to a soft dough, the softer the better.

✱ Roll the dough into a thick sausage shape and cut into 16 small balls the size of a small walnut. Drop them into the hot kidney mix and place the whole pan in the oven. This is why I specified a shallow pan.

✱ Cook for 20-30 minutes, or until the tops of the dumplings are lightly browned and crisp. The bottoms will be beautifully soft and will have soaked up the lovely kidney stew. Serve with green beans or peas.

Braised hearts with 40 cloves of garlic & chicory

THIS IS A DECEPTIVELY EASY RECIPE, JUST RELYING ON TIME AND SOME FULL-FLAVOURED INGREDIENTS. I BALANCE THE BITTERNESS OF THE CHICORY WITH A LITTLE SUGAR AND WHITE WINE. IT CAN BE COOKED IN A MODERATE OVEN, BUT WILL SIMMER AWAY QUITE HAPPILY ON THE HOB IN A PAN WITH A TIGHT-FITTING LID, ALTHOUGH YOU MAY HAVE TO TOP UP WITH BOILING WATER OCCASIONALLY. THE FINISHED DISH IS DELICIOUS AND HAS, BELIEVE IT OR NOT, A VERY MILD GARLIC FLAVOUR.

Serves 4   Preparation time 20 minutes   Cooking time 2 hours 30 minutes

4 tablespoons olive oil
4 pig's hearts, washed well and trimmed
2 large onions, roughly chopped
40 garlic cloves, peeled but left whole
2 heads of chicory, cut into 2cm pieces
300ml strong chicken or pork stock
1 medium glass or about 150ml white wine
2 tablespoons caster sugar
salt and freshly ground black pepper

✱ Heat the olive oil in a saucepan.

✱ Cut the hearts into quarters lengthways and then pat dry with kitchen paper or a clean tea-towel.

✱ Place the heart pieces in the hot oil and brown well. Next, add the onions and garlic cloves and brown again over a high heat. Add the chicory pieces and stir well.

✱ Then add the stock, wine, sugar and a good dose of salt and pepper to the pan, really mixing well.

✱ Bring to the boil, then reduce the heat right down, cover and gently simmer for a couple of hours, or until very tender. Keep an eye on the pan, topping up with boiling water if needed.

✱ Once cooked, check the seasoning and adjust if necessary. Serve with mashed potatoes and a little English or Dijon mustard.

Lightly braised liver with lettuce, peas, bacon & mint

I REMEMBER LIVER AND ONIONS AT SCHOOL: DRY, STRONG AND NOT VERY NICE. MY GOOD FRIEND IS A DEVELOPMENT CHEF AT A MAJOR READY-MEAL PRODUCER, AND LIVER AND BACON BRAISE WITH GRAVY IS ONE OF THEIR BEST SELLERS ALL YEAR ROUND. MY MUM DID A GREAT VERSION AND HER SECRET WAS NOT TO OVERCOOK THE LIVER. SLIGHTLY PINK IS THE WAY TO GO WITH ALL LIVER IN MY VIEW. HERE IS A REALLY TASTY RECIPE THAT IS VERY EASY TO COOK AND LOOKS GREAT.

Serves 4   Preparation time 25 minutes   Cooking time 20 minutes

150g unsalted butter
500g fresh pig's liver, without tubes and skin,
    cut into 8 nice pieces on a slight angle, about 2–3cm thick
6–8 tablespoons plain flour
100g smoked bacon, cut into very thin strips
1 small onion, finely chopped
200g firm lettuce, such as Cos (Romaine) or Iceberg, finely sliced
150g frozen peas
about 300ml chicken stock
    or 300ml boiling water and 10g chicken stock cube, crumbled
2–3 tablespoons chopped fresh mint
salt and freshly ground black pepper
caster sugar, to taste

✱ Heat the butter in a large sauté pan large enough to seal all the liver at the same time.

✱ Dust the liver slices with salt and pepper and then flour them well.

✱ Once the butter is foaming, add the liver slices and cook for a couple of minutes to get a nice colour. Turn over and do the same on the other side, leaving the liver still raw in the centre. Remove the liver from the pan and set aside.

✱ Add the bacon to the pan and cook until the fat is released, then add the onion and cook for a few minutes, stirring well.

✱ Add the lettuce, frozen peas and stock or water and stock cube and bring to the boil. Return the liver to the pan, turn down the heat to a simmer and cook for a couple of minutes on each side; do not overcook. The stock will thicken from the flour on the liver.

✱ Add the mint and mix well, then re-season with salt, pepper and sugar to taste. Serve straight away – the inside of the liver should be just pink.

Brain & avocado wrap

AS A YOUNG CHEF WE WOULD COOK LAMB'S AND PIG'S BRAINS ALL THE TIME – THEY WERE ALL THE RAGE IN THE 1970S. SOME YEARS AGO WHEN I VISITED FLORENCE WITH SOME GROCERY BUYERS, WE WENT TO A LOCAL RESTAURANT FOR LUNCH. THERE WERE NO MENUS, JUST A RATHER FLAMBOYANT CHEF WITH BRIGHT RED TROUSERS AND A FULL HANDLEBAR MOUSTACHE. THE FOOD ARRIVED IN WAVES, SOME GOOD AND SOME NOT SO GOOD. BUT THE THIRD COURSE WAS A LARGE FOIL PACKET THAT WAS SERVED IN THE MIDDLE OF THE TABLE. WE WERE GIVEN SMALL PLATES AND TEASPOONS. THE CHEF ARRIVED AND OPENED UP THE PACKET TO REVEAL A PERFECTLY INTACT, LIGHTLY STEAMED BRAIN. IT LOOKED LIKE SOMETHING FROM A HORROR MOVIE. IT HAD BEEN SEASONED WITH SALT, PEPPER AND NUTMEG, AND WAS SWIMMING IN BUTTER. THE WAY TO EAT IT WAS WITH A TEASPOON, GENTLY SPOONING AWAY THE WOBBLY, DELICATE FLESH. IT WAS DELICIOUS, BUT I WILL NEVER FORGET THE LOOK OF REVULSION ON SOME OF MY FELLOW GUESTS' FACES. IN THE END THEY DID ALL TRY IT, HOWEVER. IN THIS VERSION I HAVE ADDED A FEW MORE TEXTURES AND FLAVOURS, WHICH I THINK WORK REALLY WELL.

Serves 4   Preparation time 15 minutes, plus cooling/chilling   Cooking time 10 minutes

2 fresh pig's brains, washed well
300ml cold water
2 tablespoons vinegar (any type will do)
2 bay leaves
a few fresh parsley stalks
10 black peppercorns
4 tablespoons plain flour, seasoned with salt and pepper
2 large eggs, beaten
6–8 tablespoons dried breadcrumbs
4 tablespoons olive oil
salt and freshly ground black pepper

WRAPS
4 x 24cm soft flour wraps
¼ Iceberg lettuce, thinly sliced
4 large smoked streaky bacon rashers,
    cooked until very crispy
2 hard-boiled eggs, peeled and halved
4 tablespoons mayonnaise
a few fresh coriander leaves
1 avocado, peeled, stoned and sliced into 8 thin slivers
2 spring onions, finely sliced
1 carrot, peeled and finely grated (optional)

✱ Put the washed brains into a small saucepan and cover with the water. Add the vinegar, salt and pepper, bay leaves, parsley stalks and peppercorns.

✱ Bring just to the boil, then turn the brains over, turn off the heat and leave to cool completely, then chill well.

✱ Once chilled, remove the brains from the water and pat dry with kitchen paper. The brains will have set quite nicely, but not cooked through.

✱ Put the seasoned flour, beaten eggs and breadcrumbs into three separate dishes. Slice the brain into 8 small pieces and dip first into the seasoned flour, then the beaten egg and finally the breadcrumbs.

✱ Heat the olive oil in a sauté pan, add the breadcrumbed brain pieces and sauté for 2–3 minutes on each side; do not overcook. Remove from the pan and keep warm.

✱ Lay out a wrap on a chopping board. Place a little Iceberg lettuce down one end of the wrap. Top with a bacon rasher, sprinkle with a little salt and pepper and add 2 pieces of breadcrumbed brain.

✱ Next, add half a boiled egg, a tablespoon of mayo, a few coriander leaves, 2 slivers of avocado and a sprinkling of spring onions, plus carrot if you want. Fold the bottom edge over, then fold in both sides and finally roll up tightly. Repeat the process with the remaining wraps. Eat straight away.

My faggots

I DEVELOPED THIS TAKE ON A CLASSIC BRITISH DISH A LONG WHILE BACK AND IT STILL REMAINS ONE OF MY FAVOURITES. MY CHEFS AND I IN THE KITCHEN BRIGADE WOULD MAKE GAME FAGGOTS, INCLUDING A HARE VARIETY, AND THEY WOULD SELL REALLY WELL. I ADD HERBS AND GARLIC TO DEVELOP THE FLAVOUR, AND REDUCING DOWN THE STOCK THEY ARE COOKED IN MAKES A REAL DIFFERENCE. OF COURSE, THE TRADITIONAL CRUSHED PEAS AND MASH ARE THE ONLY THINGS TO SERVE WITH THEM.

Serves 4   Preparation time 30 minutes   Cooking time about 1 hour in total

500g pork belly
150g pig's liver, without tubes and skin
1 pig's heart, washed well
150g pork back fat
2 tablespoons vegetable oil
2 large onions, finely chopped
2 garlic cloves, crushed
¼ teaspoon ground nutmeg
¼ teaspoon ground mace
1 teaspoon dried sage
1 teaspoon dried thyme
4 tablespoons chopped fresh flat-leaf parsley
2 eggs, beaten
6 tablespoons Worcestershire sauce
6–8 tablespoons dried breadcrumbs
about 800ml hot well-flavoured brown pork or chicken stock
salt and freshly ground black pepper

* Finely mince the meat, offal and fat through a 5mm plate into a large bowl.

* Heat the vegetable oil in a sauté pan, then add the onions and garlic and cook for 10 minutes to soften slightly. Add the spices and cook, stirring, for a further 2 minutes, then leave to cool.

* Transfer the cooled onion and garlic mixture to a bowl, then add the minced meat mixture and mix well. Next, add all the herbs, the eggs, the Worcestershire sauce and the breadcrumbs, and season with salt and pepper.

* Mould the mixture into roughly 100g balls, about the size of a small apple. Pack into a roasting tray nice and neatly and spoon over the boiling stock until it comes three-quarters of the way up the faggots. Cover loosely with foil.

* Cook in the oven for about 30 minutes, then remove the foil and cook for a further 20 minutes to reduce the liquor slightly. You can of course thicken the gravy with a few gravy granules if you want to.

* Serve the faggots with a little of the gravy, mushy peas and mashed potatoes.

Mustard ear salad

I FIRST SERVED EARS ON MY MENU MANY YEARS AGO. IN FACT, AT THE TIME I OFFERED THEM FOR FREE TO GET GUESTS TO TRY THEM. THEY WENT DOWN REALLY WELL AND BECAME A STAPLE ON THE MENU, COOKED IN MANY DIFFERENT WAYS. THIS WAS ONE OF THE MOST POPULAR.

Serves 4   Preparation time 15 minutes, plus cooling/chilling   Cooking time about 2 hours 15 minutes in total

2 large pig's ears
10g beef stock cube, crumbled
1 celery stick, sliced
1 carrot, peeled and sliced
1 onion, sliced
3 teaspoons Dijon mustard
2 tablespoons chopped fresh basil
2 eggs, beaten
125g panko breadcrumbs*
salt and freshly ground black pepper

SALAD
1 large carrot, peeled
½ cucumber
1 small red onion, sliced
125g crunchy lettuce, such as Iceberg, sliced
½ fennel bulb, sliced into slivers

DRESSING
85ml extra virgin olive oil
2 tablespoons sherry vinegar
½ teaspoon Dijon mustard
¼ teaspoon caster sugar
grated zest of 1 and juice of ½ lemon

✱ Remove any hairs from the ears by using a kitchen blowtorch or holding over a gas flame with tongs, then wash them well.

✱ Put the pig's ears into a large pan of boiling water with the stock cube, celery, carrot and onion. Bring to the boil and season well, then reduce the heat and simmer very gently for about 2 hours until soft and tender. Top up with water if necessary.

✱ Drain the ears and leave to cool, then pat dry. Chill the ears between two plates to help flatten them.

✱ Preheat the grill to medium.

✱ Place the ears on a board and slice lengthways into thick slices. Make a paste with the mustard and basil and then coat the ear slices with the paste.

✱ Put the beaten egg and breadcrumbs into two separate dishes. Dip each ear slice into the beaten egg and then coat with the breadcrumbs.

✱ Lay the slices on a sheet of foil in a roasting tray and grill for about 5 minutes on each side until crisp and pale golden.

✱ Meanwhile, prepare the salad and dressing. Use a vegetable peeler to slice the carrot and cucumber into thin, wide strips. Put into a large bowl and add the onion, lettuce and fennel.

✱ Mix all the dressing ingredients together, then add to the salad ingredients and toss in the dressing.

✱ Place the salad on large plates, then arrange the warm, crisp ear strips on top.

*Panko breadcrumbs are a Japanese version of breadcrumbs made from crustless bread that is coarsely ground into larger flakes than regular breadcrumbs. The result is lighter and crispier.

Black pudding fritters and baby onions braised with balsamic

I LOVE BLACK PUDDING IN ANY WAY, SHAPE OR FORM, AND I HAVE ALWAYS COOKED WITH IT IN VARIOUS GUISES. I QUITE LIKE TO ADD A LITTLE TO A BRAISE OR STEW TO ADD AN EXTRA DIMENSION, OR TO A HOT POT. IT CAN WORK WELL TOO IN STUFFINGS AND SOME TERRINES, PROVIDING YOU ARE CAREFUL WITH THE AMOUNT YOU ADD. I ALSO USED TO PLACE A THIN SLIVER ON SOME TART APPLE PURÉE AND TOP WITH A FAT, JUICY ROASTED SCALLOP. HERE IT'S DEEP-FRIED AND SERVED WITH SOME BABY ONIONS BRAISED IN BALSAMIC VINEGAR TO BALANCE THE RICHNESS.

Serves 4   Preparation time 15 minutes   Cooking time 40 minutes

125g self-raising flour
pinch of salt
pinch of ground black pepper
1 heaped tablespoon chopped fresh flat-leaf parsley
about 150ml sparkling water or lager
vegetable oil, for frying
400g piece of black pudding (minimum weight), cut into 1.5cm round slices

BABY ONIONS
3 tablespoons olive oil
25g butter
2 tablespoons balsamic vinegar, plus 1 teaspoon to serve
600g baby (pickling) onions, peeled but root left on
1 tablespoon snipped fresh tarragon
sea salt and freshly ground black pepper

* Preheat the oven to 200°C/Gas 4.

* First make the onions. Put the oil, butter and balsamic vinegar into a deep baking dish. Add the whole onions (some can be halved if difficult to peel) and tumble them in the oil mixture.

* Cook, uncovered, in the oven for 30–40 minutes until the onions are soft.

* Remove the dish from the oven, and while the onions are still warm, drizzle the remaining teaspoon of balsamic over and season with salt crystals and ground black pepper. Mix the tarragon through lightly, tucking it into the onions.

* While the onions are finishing cooking, put the flour, seasoning and parsley into a small bowl and beat in the sparkling water or lager until smooth, adjusting the amount of liquid to get a loose consistency.

* Heat about 2cm vegetable oil in a large, deep pan. Dip each piece of black pudding into the batter and fry, in batches, in the hot oil for about 2 minutes on each side, turning once, until golden and crisp. Lift the fritters out with a slotted spoon and drain on kitchen paper.

* Serve the fritters hot with the braised baby onions and some fresh baby spinach leaves, simply dressed with lemon juice and cracked black pepper.

Scratchings

OVER THE YEARS, I HAVE SOUGHT TO GET THE METHOD RIGHT NOT ONLY FOR PORK SCRATCHINGS BUT FOR CRACKLING. NOW I KNOW THEY ARE DIFFERENT, BUT WHAT I HAVE FOUND IS THAT THE BASIC PRINCIPLE IS THE SAME: TO EXTRUDE AS MUCH FAT AS POSSIBLE FROM THE RIND SO THAT IT WILL CRISP UP PERFECTLY. IN THE FOLLOWING RECIPE I USE A DEHYDRATOR, BUT YOU CAN DRY THE SIMMERED RINDS ON A BAKING TRAY IN THE OVEN FOR THE SAME AMOUNT OF TIME. I DID TRY FRYING AND THEN BAKING THEM, BUT THE END RESULT WAS GREASY AND THE CRISPNESS WAS NOT EVEN ENOUGH. SO WHAT YOU NEED TO DO FIRST IS TO CUT AWAY ALL THE INNER FAT FROM THE RINDS, LEAVING 5MM AT THE MOST TO ENSURE A YIELDING, TASTY SCRATCHING. A WORD OF WARNING: THE SCRATCHINGS DO SPLUTTER WHEN BAKING IN THE OVEN, SO LOOSELY COVER WITH FOIL OR BE PREPARED TO CLEAN YOUR OVEN, BUT IT'S A SMALL PRICE TO PAY.

Serves 4   Preparation time 10 minutes   Cooking time about 3 or 6 hours in total, but trust me it's worth it

750g pork rind, with 5mm maximum depth of fat on the inside
150ml vegetable or inexpensive olive oil, or melted lard
salt and freshly ground black pepper
malt vinegar, to serve (optional)

✱ Put the pork rind into a saucepan and add a little salt.

✱ Bring to a simmer and cook until when you pinch the rind (sufficiently cooled!) your fingernails will go through it easily. This should take about 35–40 minutes. I do this so that when the scratchings are fully cooked you get an even bite, without breaking your teeth.

✱ Once the rind is ready, drain well, place on kitchen paper and dry thoroughly. Then either pop into a dehydrator set to 55–60°C and dry for 5 hours, or alternatively, place on a cake cooling rack set over a baking tray and bake in the oven preheated to 140°C/Gas 1 for a couple of hours. The scratchings will then be firmer and ready to go.

✱ Turn the oven up, or preheat, to 220°C/Gas 7 and spread the rinds out on a baking tray. Liberally drizzle with the oil or melted lard and season well with salt and pepper. Cook for about 20 minutes until crispy and well blistered, turning over only when the popping sound has stopped coming from the oven; this way you will avoid burning yourself.

✱ Remove the tray from the oven and drain the scratchings well on kitchen paper – you will find that much of the oil and fat has cooked out.

✱ Dust with salt and pepper and serve warm; not too hot. Sprinkling over a little malt vinegar at the last moment is also delicious.

Smoked bacon & snout boulangère potatoes

I HATE WASTE AND HERE IS A GREAT RECIPE FOR USING UP EVERY PART OF THE BEAST. IT'S A REALLY NICE WAY OF ADDING GREAT TEXTURE AND TASTE TO A SIMPLE POTATO DISH, AND THE END RESULT IS VERY SATISFYING.

Serves 4–6   Preparation time 20 minutes, plus standing   Cooking time about 3 hours

8 pig's snouts, washed well
1 tablespoon salt
½ tablespoon ground black pepper
500ml chicken stock or 500ml water and 2 x 10g chicken stock cubes, crumbled
150g smoked bacon or pancetta, chopped
4 large potatoes, peeled and sliced about 2cm thick
2 large onions, finely sliced
2 garlic cloves, chopped
2 tablespoons chopped fresh flat-leaf parsley
1 tablespoon chopped fresh thyme
1 tablespoon chopped fresh sage
150g butter, melted, or 150ml vegetable oil
salt and freshly ground black pepper

✱ Put the snouts into a non-metallic bowl or dish, sprinkle with the 1 tablespoon salt and ½ tablespoon pepper and leave to stand for a couple of hours in a cool place, or overnight in the fridge.

✱ When ready to cook, rinse well under cold water and put into a small saucepan. Cover with the stock or water and stock cubes and add the bacon or pancetta. Bring to the boil, then reduce the heat and simmer for 1 hour, or until the snouts are tender and very soft.

✱ Lift out the snouts with a slotted spoon and chop into small pieces. Measure the stock and make up to 750ml.

✱ Preheat the oven to 220°C/Gas 7.

✱ Put the potatoes, onions, garlic, herbs, salt and pepper and snouts into a bowl and really mix well. Pack into a 30 x 35cm baking dish with sides 6cm deep.

✱ Bring the stock and bacon or pancetta to the boil and then pour over the potato mixture. Press down well and cover with foil. Place on a baking tray and bake for 1 hour, or until the potatoes are soft.

✱ Remove the tray from the oven and then remove the foil from the dish – the smell will be fabulous. Drizzle the melted butter or oil over the potatoes and gently press down with a potato masher.

✱ Return to the oven, uncovered, for about 15–20 minutes until the stock is reduced and the potatoes and snouts are nicely glazed.

✱ Remove from the oven, re-press and serve as a main on its own, or as an accompaniment to any pork dish.

Twice-cooked ears Chinese style with noodles

PIG'S EARS HAVE A LOVELY GELATINOUS TEXTURE AND FLAVOUR THAT IS VERY HARD TO DESCRIBE. THEY WORK WELL IN ALL SORTS OF WAYS, SUCH AS IN STEWS, SALADS, SOUPS AND EVEN SLIGHTLY SALTED AND CURED OVERNIGHT TO MAKE A LOVELY CONFIT. THEY ARE ALSO GREAT CRISPED UP IN THE OVEN WITH A SMEAR OF MUSTARD AND A CRUNCHY COATING OF BREADCRUMBS (SEE PAGE 185), OR IN A STIR-FRY WITH LOTS OF VEGETABLES WITH A SHARP SAUCE, AND HERE I'VE GIVEN THEM THE FULL CHINESE TREATMENT. DO TRY THESE RECIPES – I'M SURE YOU WILL BE PLEASANTLY SURPRISED.

Serves 4   Preparation time 25 minutes, plus cooling/chilling   Cooking time 2 hours 15 minutes

2 large pig's ears
10g beef stock cube, crumbled
1 celery stick, sliced
1 carrot, peeled and sliced
1 onion, sliced
2 tablespoons hoisin sauce
2 tablespoons dark soy sauce
2 teaspoons sweet chilli sauce
2 teaspoons rice wine vinegar
2 teaspoons runny honey
1 teaspoon Chinese five-spice powder
1 teaspoon cornflour

NOODLES
125g small broccoli florets (including stems), sliced
125g dried rice noodles
1 teaspoon sesame oil
1 tablespoon vegetable oil
150g shiitake or brown cap mushrooms, sliced
1 garlic clove, chopped
2 spring onions, sliced
225g can sliced bamboo shoots or water chestnuts, drained
3 tablespoons oyster sauce
3 tablespoons light soy sauce
3 tablespoons water
salt

✱ Remove any hairs from the pig's ears by using a kitchen blowtorch or holding over a gas flame with tongs, then wash them well.

✱ Put the ears into a large pan of boiling water with the stock cube, celery, carrot and onion. Return to the boil, then reduce the heat and simmer very gently for about 2 hours until soft and tender. Top up with water if necessary.

✱ Drain the ears and leave to cool, then pat dry. Chill the ears between two plates to help flatten them.

✱ Preheat the oven to 190°C/Gas 5.

✱ Place the ears on a sheet of foil in a roasting tray. Mix the remaining ingredients for the ears to a smooth paste and use to coat the ears evenly.

✱ Roast the ears in the oven for about 15 minutes until nicely glazed. You may need to recoat with the juices a couple of times.

✱ Remove from the oven, place on a board and chop into large pieces.

✱ While the ears are roasting, add the broccoli to a pan of boiling salted water and cook for 2 minutes.

✱ Lift out of the pan with a slotted spoon and set aside. Pour the hot cooking water over the rice noodles in a bowl to cover and leave to stand for 3 minutes. Drain the noodles and then stir the sesame oil through them.

✱ Heat a large frying pan or wok and add the vegetable oil. When hot, add the mushrooms and stir-fry for 5 minutes. Add the garlic and spring onions and stir-fry for 2 minutes, then stir in the drained bamboo shoots or water chestnuts, oyster sauce, soy sauce and water.

✱ Finally, mix in the rice noodles and continue to cook for another couple of minutes until warmed through.

✱ Serve the noodles in deep bowls and top with the chunks of pig's ear; I sometimes mix the ears through the noodles.

Roasted stuffed pig's head with pistachios, dates & parsley ⫸⟶

Roasted stuffed pig's head with pistachios, dates & parsley

WHEN I WAS A YOUNG CHEF WE USED WHOLE PIG'S HEADS ON BUFFETS ALL THE TIME. THEY WOULD BE ROASTED OR POACHED AND THEN STUFFED WITH ALL MANNER OF THINGS FROM TRUFFLES TO CURED MEATS AND FRUITS. THE CHRISTMAS BUFFET ALWAYS HAD A STUFFED HEAD COATED IN A SHINY BLACK GLAZE, THE EYES AND TUSKS DEPICTED WITH PIPED WHIPPED BUTTER – ALL VERY STRIKING. MY FATHER ALWAYS LOVED BRAWN, MADE FROM BOILING THE HEAD WITH TROTTERS, REMOVING THE MEAT AND SETTING IT IN THE FANTASTIC JELLY. THIS RECIPE IS DELICIOUS, AND THE CHANCES ARE THE BUTCHER MAY EVEN GIVE YOU THE PIG'S HEAD FOR FREE. GOOD LUCK!

Serves 8–10   Preparation time 40 minutes   Cooking time 2 hours 30–40 minutes, plus resting

1 boneless pig's head, in one piece (the butcher may make a small charge for boning the head)
1.5kg minced pork
2 onions, finely chopped
6 garlic cloves, crushed
2 eggs, beaten
2 heaped tablespoons roughly chopped fresh thyme
200g dates (Medjool are perfect), chopped
100g skinned pistachio nuts
grated zest and juice of 2 large limes
salt and freshly ground black pepper

GLAZE
150ml runny honey
juice of 2 large lemons
pinch of salt

✻ Preheat the oven to 160°C/Gas 3.

✻ Open the head up and remove any scraps of fat or bloody parts.

✻ Mix the minced pork, onions, garlic and eggs together well in a large bowl, then add the thyme, dates, pistachios and lemon zest and juice. Season well with salt and pepper and really mix well.

✻ Place the stuffing in the head cavity and gently roll up. This is the most important bit. Using a trussing needle and strong string, start under the snout and carefully sew up the bottom and around the back of the head until you have sealed it well.

✻ Reshape the head so it roughly resembles a real head again. You can lightly pack around the head with foil to keep the shape, but I wouldn't bother too much.

✻ Place the head in a large baking tray and season all over with salt and pepper. Using a large piece of foil, double or triple wrap the ears and the snout to stop them from burning. Roast in the oven for 2 hours.

✻ Remove the head from the oven – it will be nicely browned and looking good. Remove the foil from the ears and the snout. Mix the glaze ingredients together well, then use a pastry brush to brush all over the head.

✻ Return to the oven and roast for a further 30–40 minutes, basting every 5-6 minutes until well browned.

✻ Once cooked, remove from the oven, loosely cover with foil and leave to rest for 45 minutes. Then slice and enjoy – the lovely gelatinous meat and membranes, accompanied by the fruity stuffing, is worth all that effort and cooking.

Bitter chocolate blood & orange pot

I HAD A VERSION OF THIS MANY YEARS AGO IN A SMALL TOWN IN ITALY. IT WAS THE FINALE TO A STUNNING MEAL THAT BEGAN WITH A BOILED RABBIT SUBMERGED IN WARM, SAGE-FLAVOURED EXTRA VIRGIN OLIVE OIL. THE LARGE BOWL WAS PASSED AROUND THE RESTAURANT FOR ALL THE DINERS TO HELP THEMSELVES. NEXT CAME A TINY PEASANT DISH OF BRAISED COCKSCOMBS, HEARTS, SWEETBREADS, SMALL VEGETABLES AND VEAL TENDONS, ALL IN A SHARP, SLIGHTLY VINEGARY SAUCE – DELICIOUS. TO FINISH, WE WERE SERVED A DESSERT OF BITTER CHOCOLATE FLAVOURED WITH EXTRA VIRGIN OLIVE OIL AND THICKENED WITH FRESH PIG'S BLOOD – WOW... HERE IS MY VERSION; I SHALL LEAVE IT UP TO YOU TO REACH YOUR OWN VERDICT.

Serves 6–8   Preparation time 15 minutes, plus cooling/chilling   Cooking time 15 minutes

700ml milk
200g bitter chocolate (70 per cent cocoa solids is perfect), broken up into small pieces
175g caster sugar
50g dried pig's blood
2g salt
50ml extra virgin olive oil
finely grated zest of ½ large orange

✱ Put the milk, chocolate and sugar into a saucepan and gently warm, stirring all the time, until the chocolate is half melted.

✱ Add the pig's blood and salt and whisk well. Stir until the chocolate has fully melted and you have a nice shiny sauce.

✱ Bring just up to boiling point, then remove from the heat and leave to cool for 2 minutes. Stir well and then add the olive oil and orange zest. You may need to pass the mixture through a fine sieve, depending on the blood used.

✱ Pour into 6–8 small ramekins or glasses. Leave to cool completely, then chill well. Serve with a shortbread or crisp sweet biscuit and a little lightly whipped double cream dusted with grated chocolate.

GLOSSARY

Air-dried
A generic term describing a product that has been cured and undergone a lengthy maturation period. How long this maturation takes depends on the thickness of the product, so the thinner it is the quicker it will be.

Bread rusk
A form of breadcrumb commonly used to help bind and provide texture to a sausage. It will also soak up twice its weight in water.

Brine
A solution of water and curing salt used primarily for curing bacon and ham.

Natural casings
The small intestine of pigs, sheep or cattle, which, cleaned and brined (salted), is used to make a whole host of products from chipolatas to salami.

Curing salt
Salt that has been blended with a curing agent. For salami production, for example, it often contains 0.6% sodium nitrite.

Deadweight
The term used to describe the carcass weight of any animal that has been slaughtered.

Dextrose
Commercial glucose, commonly used in the production of salamis.

Fat content
The amount of fat required to make a product. Within the trade, cuts of meat are bought according to how much visual lean meat (%vl) is needed.

Fee (emulsifying agent)
Typically, e471, the mono and diglyceride fatty acid commonly used as an emulsifier and stabiliser in pâté-like products.

Hot smoked
A product that is cooked in a smoke-filled environment, typically at temperatures of between 75 and 85°C. Any kind of hardwood can be used for this process.

Lactic acid
One of the by-products of fermentation in a salami. Lactobacillus and pediococcus bacteria metabolise (feed on) the sugar content and produce lactic acid.

Pave
Hog casing that has been dried and formed into sheets so it can be wrapped around products such as coppa and lomo.

pH Meter/pH
A device that accurately measures acidic and alkaline levels. A must-have for food safety if you are producing salami or any other fermented product.

Potassium nitrate

More commonly known as saltpetre, this is used as a curing agent in curing salt. Its use is strictly regulated and it is always best to source from reputable suppliers who will certify how much has been used.

Reddening

The term commonly used to describe the fermentation process in salamis. They start off a dismal grey colour and after the starter cultures have worked their magic they turn a lovely red colour.

Relative humidity

The ratio of partial pressure of water vapour in an air–water mixture to the saturated vapour pressure of water at a certain temperature. It's particularly relevant in the production of salamis and air-dried products.

Saltpetre

See Potassium nitrate.

Sodium ascorbate

The salt of ascorbic acid. Mostly used as a curing accelerator and anti-oxidant. It is typically used in all products that are made with curing salt.

Sodium nitrite

Used as a curing agent in curing salt, for example in the production of salamis.

Sous vide

The French term for 'under vacuum', it is a method of cooking whereby food is sealed in airtight bags and cooked in water at lower temperatures and for longer periods of time than in conventional cooking.

Starter culture

Bacteria such as lactobacillus that feed on sugars and produce lactic acid. Used in the fermentation process, it is responsible for giving salami its distinctive flavour and for lowering the pH value of the product.

Tempered

Frozen meat that has been placed in a fridge and allowed to soften.

Vacuum cooking

See Sous vide.

STOCKISTS & USEFUL INFORMATION

Meat & ingredients

The Best Butchers
Simon Boddy's butchery.
www.thebestbutchers.co.uk
Unit 5, Lower Rectory Farm, Great
Brickhill, Milton Keynes.
01908 375275

Continental Meat Technology
Seasonings, functional ingredients,
herbs and spices for sausages, hams,
bacon, cooked and cured meats,
including the specialist flavourings
mentioned in this book.
www.continentalmeattechnology.co.uk
01908 584489

Weschenfelder
Sausage making supplies, from casings
and seasonings to mincers, knives and
smoking machines.
www.weschenfelder.co.uk

Smoking & curing equipment

Arden Smoker Supplies
www.foodsmoker.co.uk

Bradley Smoker
www.bradleysmoker.co.uk

Hot Smoked
www.hotsmoked.co.uk

PH Meters and Food Thermometers
www.digital-meters.com
www.thermometer.co.uk

Wood-fired ovens

Kilnlinings
www.kilnlinings.co.uk

The Stone Bake Oven Company
www.thestonebakeovencompany.co.uk

Wood-fired Oven
www.wood-firedoven.co.uk

Advice & support on keeping pigs

**Department for Environment, Food
and Rural Affairs** (Defra)
Crucial information including how to
register as a pig keeper, welfare rules
and guidance and requirements for
keeping and transporting pigs.
www.gov.uk/defra

The British Pig Association
www.britishpigs.org.uk

National Pig Association
www.npa-uk.org.uk

Australia

www.butcherathome.com.au

www.australianpigfarmers.com.au

**Department of Agriculture, Fisheries
and Forestry** (DAFF)
www.daff.gov.au

New Zealand

www.bradleysmoker.co.nz

www.thecasingboutique.co.nz

www.kitchenshop.co.nz

New Zealand Pork
www.nzpork.co.nz

Ministry for Primary Industries (MPI)
www.mpi.govt.nz

South Africa

www.thebutcherweb.co.za

www.crownnational.co.za

**Department for Agriculture, Forestry
and Fisheries**
www.nda.agric.za

INDEX

A book doesn't just happen, and there are a few people we would really like to thank.

Firstly Kyle, for giving us the opportunity to get nearly 60 years of work between us into written form. It was a lot of hard work all round, so thanks also to our fabulous KB team: editor Judith Hannam, who always has a smile on her face, copy editor Jo Richardson, editorial assistant Tara O'Sullivan and designer Helen Bratby.

My now retired and very much missed agent, Mr John Rush, and my not-retired-just-yet agent Luigi Bonomi. Thank you gentlemen.

The photographs are outstanding, so huge thanks to Peter Cassidy for all the hours laying in mud, pig poo and even snow to get the right shots.

Thanks also to food stylist Mima Sinclair for some stunning looking dishes and Iris Bromet for styling.

My pig fascination started at a very early age with the late Mr George King. He taught me that good meat comes from happy, well-fed, well looked after pigs, and that has never left me. Thanks to my baby brother Mike for all the graft in setting up and helping over the years, top man. Later in life another person fired me up again – Peter Gott. His knowledge is second to none and he has always been at the end of the phone when I've needed help! John Rickatson, the affable Yorkshire man who breeds an amazing pig, thank you also. Please keep going! And to Mr Paul Gutteridge, who helps me. I would struggle without him; he also doubles up as chief taster!

Finally Simon Boddy. He really is the man, not often I say that.
Phil Vickery

To Phil, a massive thank you for giving me the opportunity to help with this book. I have loved every minute. Also to Peter Cassidy and the team at Kyle Books for turning a shared passion into something truly wonderful. It was a pleasure to work with such incredibly clever and talented people – amazing! Simon Boddy

oink